A HISTORICAL NARRATIVE OF
LADY FATIMA BINT MUHAMMAD

FATIMA

THE FLOWER OF LIFE

JALAL MOUGHANIA

Fatima: The Flower of Life

Author: Jalal Moughania

© 2024 The Mainstay Foundation

Calligraphy cover design: Zuhair Hussaini

Printed in the United States.

ISBN: 978-1943393480

To the woman upon whose shoulders Islam rose and God's name was heard. Lady Fatima's Mother and the Beloved of the Seal of Prophets Muhammad...

The Princess of Quraysh
The Mother of the Believers
Lady Khadija bint Khuwaylid

Peace be upon Fatima

And her father the Seal

Peace be upon Fatima

And her mother the Great

Peace be upon Fatima

And her husband the Prince

Peace be upon Fatima

And her sons the Heirs

Peace be upon Fatima

And the Divine Secret

Peace be upon Fatima

CONTENTS

NOTES ON USAGE, SPELLING AND FORMATTING

In writing this book, I have elected to use more familiar English spellings for names of figures and subjects and have done so without diacritical marks. Thus, you will see Ali instead of 'Ali and Umar instead of 'Umar.

In addition, for the sake of fluidity, I have limited the use of honorary titles for the Holy Prophet Muhammad and his Household, such as Imam Husayn and Lady Zaynab, peace be upon them all. Therefore, you will see that most of the text will refer to them simply by their first name: Hasan, Husayn, Zaynab, etc.

I have also limited the use of their full names, such as Ali ibn Abi Talib and Fatima bint Muhammad, to avoid the "Russian novel effect", keeping in mind the English reader who may be more easily confused with multiple unfamiliar names. There are times that the full names, or the second part of the names, are used to either distinguish between personalities with similar names, such as Abdullah ibn Abbas and Abdullah ibn Umar in the same conversation. They may also be used at times to emphasize the individual's parentage or lineage.

Furthermore, though "Koran" is often used in English works, I have elected to use the more proper spelling of "Quran" to differentiate between the *qaf* and *kaf* in the Arabic, which, if confused, could render different meanings of the word.

The reader should note that the supplication of *salawat* (a prayer asking God to send His peace and blessings upon Muhammad and the household of Muhammad) and salutations (peace be upon them) are usually recited at the mention of the Holy Prophet and his family. This is normally marked in elaborate calligraphy in Arabic text, or with (s), (a), or a similar mark in English text. Such marks do not appear in this book, so as not to disturb the flow of the reader. Nonetheless, the reader is encouraged to recite such prayers in their honor for the blessings of their mentioning.

It is worthy of note that I also relied on the English translation of Ali Quli Qara'i when citing the verses of the Holy Quran throughout this book, with minor adaptations. Wherever verses of the Quran are mentioned throughout the text, even in dialogue, I have tried my best to include the chapter and verse number; they will appear as such (5:55).

Moreover, I have italicized Arabic words, other than the names of individuals, when they first appear in the book.

In translating dialogue, I opted for utilizing an idiomizing translation (see: Dickins, Hervey, and Higgins, *Thinking Arabic Translation*, p. 15 (2nd Edition, 2017)). Thus, I opted at times to sacrifice some equivalency and detail in the translation, in favor of providing a more natural and flowing text.

Moreover, while I attempted to be as faithful as possible to the information provided in the sources I relied on, this book does contain some natural dramatization of the subject historical events, without straying from the historical accounts. For example, the reader will see that some characters are portrayed as 'smiling' or 'crying,' even though some particular historical accounts may not mention their emotional state or the particularity of smiling or crying. Without these minor expressions and/or dramatizations, it may be difficult for the common reader to fully appreciate the historical narrative and understand its emotional context.

I would also like to make a few notes regarding formatting, particularly the formatting of dialogue in this book. There is a lot of dialogue in this narrative, intentionally delivered as such to give the reader the experience of witnessing the conversations that shaped such events in history. For parts of quoted content that is in the form of a sermon, monologues, lengthy prayers, or letters, the words of the speaker appear in the form of an indented and italicized block quote. Short quotes, such as those recalled from the Prophet about Fatima, are also shown in this particular format with the intention of emphasis.

The paragraphs of quoted dialogue are indented, otherwise all other paragraphs do not have indentation with the absence of dialogue in said paragraphs to distinguish between dialogue and non-dialogue text.

I pray that these choices make the book more reader friendly to the intended audience, the English-speaking reader.

Any mistakes or shortcomings are mine alone.

PREFACE

"Whenever I looked at Fatima, my sorrows would fade away."

– Imam Ali ibn Abi Talib

Lady Fatima lived during the most crucial years of Muslim history. She was raised by her father during the era in which his early community of followers faced persistent persecution before migration. Fatima would marry the champion of the Muslims, Ali ibn Abi Talib, at the peak of Islam's rise during the Prophet's lifetime. From that marriage would come the Prophet's descendants – Hasan and Husayn – a lineage that has survived to the present day. She witnessed her father's death that inevitably came with a new era of power in the newly founded Muslim nation – the Caliphate. After an attack on her own home in the Caliphate's struggle to quell any opposition to its new reign, Fatima would die only a few short months after her father the Prophet.

I wrote this historical narrative in hopes of captivating the reader to continue to learn about the features of Lady Fatima's life and the attributes of her legendary personality. She was giving, selfless, and far beyond her years. She was the "Mother of her Father". How a small girl could care for her father, physically tending to his wounds and emotionally cradling him in her little arms – while he was the greatest man to walk God's earth – is fathomable only because she was... Fatima.

In my research of the life and legacy of Lady Fatima, I benefited from several books including some original Arabic works as well as some later English translations. The following are a few that especially played a role in shaping this narrative: Shaykh Abbas Qummi's House of Sorrows, the Life of Sayyidah Fatimah al-Zahra and Her Grief; Allamah Baqir Sharif al-Qurashi's The Life of Fatima Az-Zahra': The Principal of All Women, Study and Analysis; Yousuf Lalljee's Ali the Magnificent, Sayyid Muhammad Kadhim al-Qazwini's Fatimah al-Zahra: from the Cradle to the Grave; as well as the many references used by the scholars of those works which cite to primary sources in both Sunni and Shia traditions.

It is important to note that much of the writing process involved reading the sermons of Lady Fatima, notably in the last few months of her life. The level of public advocacy she undertook in that short period of time was enough to provide generations of knowledge and wisdom into the mission and vision of Islam's Prophet Muhammad. Because of the power of her words, the reader will notice that I included such sermons in their entirety with little descriptive interference. My intention here was to preserve the integrity of those speeches and allow the words of Lady Fatima to tell their own story. This will be seen mostly in the later chapters of the book.

The nature of her tragic death speaks to one of the primary reasons I wrote this book. Her tragedy was so quick, so shocking. Her life ended so abruptly. Yet her light and legacy timeless. At the tender age of 18 (some historians say 27 on account of conflicting reports to the year of her birth), the most gracious woman would pass. How? What is more tragic is the fact that so many of us do not know the full story of her short life. Hence, the inspiration to write this book. To paint a window, just one, into her life and death.

Certainly, given the individuals involved in the history of Lady Fatima's life and death, and the role these characters play in the conscious of every Muslim, regardless of sect or school of thought, it added yet another challenge. In no way is the telling of the story of Fatima's life and death meant to disrespect or disparage any esteemed personalities in any school of thought. Rather, the story of Fatima is told to bring light to the realities and implications of individuals' choices, even with arguably noble intentions. Her story is meant to inspire and empower us to seek truth, justice, and virtue. Lady Fatima inspires us to continue on the noble path of her father – seeking excellence and soaring in virtue to the Heavens.

At the death of the Holy Prophet Muhammad, the nation surely did not experience a smooth transition of power. There was conflict. There was division. There was turmoil. And it took place amongst the chief companions, from the Muhajiroun and the Ansar. There was a struggle for power and different motivations, and perspectives of what was best for the community and who should be at the helm had huge implications on the fate of the Muslim nation. Fatima's short life would end during this sensitive period as she witnessed the establishment of the new power structure in the Caliphate that replaced her father.

It was difficult for me to write this book. Who am I to write a book about the life of the Prophet's most beloved? I am no one. That is not a statement of humility, it's a reality before the grace of Fatima. Even as I finished writing these pages, I hesitated to submit the book to its next stage in the publication process.

Of course, there are always natural hesitations when it comes to presenting your work to anyone. None of us are free from the base insecurities that exist when presenting our work, which sometimes begins to feel like an actual part of our own self, on display. But it was not like that for this work. It was different. It was much less about my work, and more about her story. As I wrote page after page, that notion deepened.

And even now, years after I began this project, I still hesitate before the grace of Fatima. I want the reader to know that I am asking her forgiveness, first and foremost, for any shortcomings towards her in this work. I know what I offer here will not do her story justice. But I earnestly pray that this humble work is a step in the direction of honoring what deserves the most honor – the excellence and virtue of Lady Fatima and her incredible legacy.

Death tells us a lot about life. Wisdom dictates that we do not ignore it. Tales of death should not be swept under the rug, especially the deaths of history's most notable figures. Lady Fatima is indeed on top of that list. Regardless of what the reader does with this story after reading it, at the very least, reflect on it. Embrace Fatima – the Flower of Life – and allow her the chance to open your eyes to the universe within you. Let her story be your guide as you journey toward the Heavens.

CHAPTER 1

LIGHT WAS BORN OF LIGHT

Surely, we have given you (Muhammad) abundance of good (al-Kawthar). Therefore, turn to your lord in prayer and sacrifice. Indeed, your enemy is the one who is without prosperity.

– Holy Quran 108:1-3

She opened her eyes and saw the world. The angels of Heaven sang, and the mortals of Earth bowed before her grace. The wind blew a breeze of Paradise and the trees of Mecca danced in celebration. The Lady of Light came into the world and gazed upon God's creation. What an honor, rather the greatest honor to have Fatima gaze upon the world. Her beautiful eyes were met by the love that all of creation came from and for. With his heavenly eyes, he gazed back. Their eyes locked, for light had created light and she was that light in his eyes. She was the starlight of Muhammad's night and the sunny warmth of his blessed day.

The Meccans mocked him for his lack of sons. They ridiculed him, in that he would have no lineage. For his wife, Lady Khadija, did in fact give him sons. But they did not survive the arid air of this life more than mere months after birth. It was God's will. Muhammad would have a progeny, without a doubt. He was God's final prophet and divine messenger, indeed. Yet, it would be through him, God's most prized and beloved creation, that God's message would be honored and protected. Muhammad would bear a progeny, legacy-makers, and viceroys of God's kingdom to bring humanity to their God given purpose – excellence.

> *"Surely we have given you (Muhammad) abundance of good (al-Kawthar). Therefore, turn to your lord in prayer and sacrifice. Indeed, your enemy is the one who is without prosperity."* (108:1-3)

Al-Kawthar, the precious Fatima. Through this revelation, God reassured his beloved Muhammad. He rejoiced with his precious baby girl and smiled in the face of the scornful. They mocked him for being sonless, but he smiled.

The Kingdom of Heaven would have its princes, and Fatima would be their queen. She would bear their light, a light that would radiate to the ends of space and time. Though her life in this world would be short, she would have a beautiful impact, a profound bearing, and a legacy like no other. In every way, an unmatched moral template for both men and women.

In the arms of revelation, Lady Fatima was cradled, and by the best of parents any child could ask for. Her father was Prophet Muhammad and her mother was Lady Khadija. The love that formed the marriage of Muhammad and Khadija radiated its light into Fatima, so that she would be the Maiden of the World, the Lady of the Light and the Flower of Life.

Decades after her lifetime, the great grandson of Lady Fatima, Ja'far Al-Sadiq, was asked about how his heavenly mother was born. He relayed the story to his companions with his prophetic smile.

> When Lady Khadija married the Prophet of God, the women of Mecca distanced themselves from her. They would not visit her house and prevented any of the women from visiting her as well. They even refused to greet Khadija when they crossed her path. Due to this, Khadija was frightful and extremely distressed, lest they also harm the Prophet. However, when Khadija became pregnant with Fatima, her unborn child would speak to her mother from the womb and console her – something which Khadija concealed from the Prophet.
>
> One day the Prophet entered the house and heard Khadija speaking with someone and inquired with his wife, 'Who are you speaking to?' Khadija replied, 'The child in my womb speaks to me and is my companion.' The Prophet continued, 'Gabriel informs me that this child is a daughter, a chaste and auspicious child, and very soon God will multiply my progeny through her and the divinely appointed leaders (Imams) will emerge from her progeny and will be made the vicegerents and my heirs after the end of revelation (i.e. after my death).

Lady Khadija spent her days like this until her beautiful Fatima would arrive and light up her world with her heavenly smile. As time drew closer to Fatima's birth, Khadija called for the women of her tribe to help her through labor. That was the custom. It was part of Arabian tradition that a woman's tribe and all those around her would flock to assist her in her delivery and the celebration of her child's birth. For Khadija, however, her invitation fell on deaf ears. The woman of Quraysh reprimanded her for not listening to them. They wanted nothing to do with her after she married Muhammad, the orphan of Abdullah whom Abu Talib took under his care.

They said that Muhammad was not of her caliber. Khadija deserved someone who was wealthy and of a prestigious stature, they said. Her essence within told her otherwise. Khadija knew that there was no match for her other than Muhammad, and that he would be the keeper of her heart until death would do them apart. And so, the women kept their distance from Khadija even when she went into childbirth. The Prophet had gained so many enemies in the earliest days of his message, that even when it came to their baby being born, only a few people would stand by their side. Joyous was Abu Talib and his blessed sons for their cousin Muhammad and his Lady Khadija. Those few would become the ones whom Fatima would love, and upon whose shoulders Islam would rise.

But Khadija was not left without sisterly support. Her Lord did not forsake her, nor did she lose hope in His benevolence. When the pangs of labor grew stronger and she had no women to comfort her, God sent her the most noble of women to be by her side. They were tall, golden in complexion, and in some ways looked like the women of Banu Hashem, but certainly were not the same.

Puzzled by these women who suddenly entered her room, Khadija asked them who they were. She was not frightened or startled by them. Instead, she was intrigued and knew they served a godly purpose. They gazed at Khadija with their angelic smiles.

O' Khadija, do not be grieved! We have come to your aid by the command of God. We are your sisters, I am Sarah the wife of Prophet Ibrahim; this is Asia, the daughter of Muzahim, the believing wife of Pharaoh, who shall be your companion in Paradise; while this is Maryam, the daughter of Imran; and the fourth one is Kulthum, the sister of Prophet Moses. God the Almighty has sent us to assist you at the time of childbirth.

Khadija let out a sigh of relief, overcome by gratitude for the gifts of God and His beautiful grace. Her sisters gathered around her, each taking a seat to her right, left, at her feet and one behind her head. They held her hands, embraced her with their heavenly presence, and helped her bring the pride and joy she would call Fatima into this world. When Fatima arrived, her light shone into every house of Mecca. There was nothing that the light of Fatima did not touch. She filled the Earth with her beauty and grace, a gift from God to humankind.

Ten maidens of Heaven would descend to the house of Khadija holding in their hands pitchers of water. The water was from the pond of Al-Kawthar in Paradise. The pond's name would later be given to Fatima as an attribute of her own. The maidens washed her with the heavenly water and wrapped her little body with two pieces of cloth. The cloth was whiter than milk and smelled sweeter than musk and amber. The newborn was completely wrapped and covered in the cloth. Then, the women asked her to speak. But how could a newborn child speak, having been only minutes in this world?

"I bear witness that there is no god but Allah, and that my father Muhammad is the Messenger of Allah," the newborn Fatima replied.

Just as Jesus the son of Mary spoke, Fatima the daughter of Muhammad would also speak. The beauty in their speech was beyond the miracle of words, it was in their praise for those who brought them into this world. They all smiled at the precious Fatima and handed her over to her mother Khadija.

"Take hold of your child, who is chaste, virtuous and filled with prosperity and auspiciousness, and a blessed progeny will emerge from her," they said to Khadija.

The world was filled with a light of joy that only Fatima could shine. The angels sang, their echoes rang across the Heavens, and God's creation praised Him for His grace upon them. Khadija held her daughter in her arms and experienced a happiness that no words could describe.

Prophet Muhammad rushed home to greet his new baby girl. Walking into the room and seeing his beloved wife Khadija holding their newborn, he beamed with his unending smile. Eagerly taking his daughter from his darling wife, Muhammad held her in his arms and kissed her. He then recited the adhan, the first call to prayer, in her right ear. He proceeded to recite the iqama, the second call to prayer, in her left ear. The very first words that she heard were the praises of God and in the voice of His Messenger.

The Prophet proceeded to give his baby girl her blessed name, "Fatima". When asked why the name Fatima, the Prophet replied, "Because she and her followers are weaned from fire," he said. Fire cannot reach Fatima and her followers.

The Holy Prophet Muhammad spoke of the blessedness and purity of his daughter Fatima. Her conception was heavenly in every sense of the word, as she was conceived through the fruit of Paradise.

> When I was carried to the Heavens during my ascensions, Gabriel took me by the hand and led me into Paradise. He then gave me some dates of Heaven and I ate them, and they became assimilated into my blood. When I returned to Earth, I approached Khadija and later she became pregnant with Fatima. Therefore, Fatima is a heavenly maiden and whenever I desire to smell the fragrance of Paradise, I smell the fragrance of my daughter Fatima.

Later in his life, the Prophet would also speak of this. Aisha would describe a conversation she had with him about Fatima. She wondered what was so special about his daughter, and why the Prophet treated her differently. Aisha said,

> I often saw the Prophet of God kiss Fatima. So, I said, 'Oh Messenger of God, I see you doing something that you did not do before.' The Prophet quickly replied, 'Oh Humayra! The night that I was carried to the

Heavens and taken to Paradise, I stood next to a tree, more beautiful than any other tree in Paradise. Its leaves were more brilliant and its fruits more delightful than any other. Then I took a fruit from that tree and ate it; it became part of my blood. When I returned to Earth, I approached Khadija, and she became pregnant with Fatima. Whenever I desire to smell the fragrance of Paradise, I smell the fragrance of Fatima.'

The fruits of Heaven that the Prophet ate came with further detail. One day, the Prophet was seated with his companions at a place named Al-Abtah which was centered between Mecca and Mena. In his company were his cousin Ali ibn Abi Talib, uncle Abbas bin Abdulmuttalib, uncle Hamza bin Abdulmuttalib, and companions Ammar bin Yasser, Abu Bakr and Umar. During their gathering, Angel Gabriel descended upon the Prophet. Gabriel appeared in his natural grandeur with his magnanimous wings stretching from east to west. Gabriel bowed before the grace of God's beloved Muhammad.

"O Muhammad! God the Almighty sends you greetings. He commands you to distance yourself from Khadija for forty days." Muhammad loved Khadija. She was the apple of his eyes and the light of his day. Thus, it was difficult to bear the idea of not spending his nights with his love. But God's commands were dearer to him than anything in creation. So, the Prophet obliged and separated from Khadija for forty days. He consumed his days in fasting and spent his nights in worship. He remained patient until the final days of that period came to a close. During this time, he sent a message to his beloved Khadija with his trusted companion Ammar bin Yaser.

The letter read in part:

> My dear Khadija, do not presume that I have distanced myself from you due to lack of love or heedlessness. Rather, my Lord has commanded me to do this so that He may manifest His will. Do not imagine anything else except fairness and felicity. God the Exalted praises you abundantly and daily in the presence of His esteemed angels. When it becomes dark, close your door and rest on the bed, and behold that I have taken abode in the house of Fatima bint Asad.

Fatima bint Asad was the wife of the Prophet's uncle, Abu Talib. It was in their home that the Prophet grew up after having been orphaned of his father, mother and even grandfather by the tender age of eight. His grandfather's name was Abdulmuttalib. Before he passed, Abdulmuttalib tasked his son Abu Talib with the care of the young Muhammad. He welcomed the task and raised him, along with his wife Fatima bint Asad, as his own.

And so, the Prophet returned at this crucial time to the home that he grew up in. He let Khadija know of his whereabouts and explained to her that there is a true purpose behind this. Though she understood and met the challenge of being apart with great patience, Lady Khadija was still heavy-hearted with the situation. Separation for such a period from her beloved was no easy task. Muhammad was everything to her.

When the forty days were over, Angel Gabriel descended again upon the Prophet.

"Allah sends greetings to you and says that you must prepare yourself for the recompense and gift," Gabriel said to the Messenger.

"What is the gift from God?" the Prophet asked Gabriel.

Gabriel did not have an answer for him.

Suddenly, Angel Michael descended from the Heavens and appeared before Gabriel and Muhammad. He came holding a golden tray covered by a cloth woven of fine silk and placed it before the Holy Prophet.

Gabriel then said, "Allah commands you to break your fast tonight with this meal."

The Prophet's cousin, Imam Ali, would describe the events at the time.

> *The Prophet had taken abode at our house. At the time of breaking his fast, he would command me to open the doors so that anyone could come in and partake in the food with him. But that night, the Prophet commanded me to stand at the door of the house and said, 'O son of Abu Talib! Consuming this meal is forbidden upon anyone except for me.'*
>
> *I sat at the door and the Prophet entered therein alone, and when he uncovered the tray, he saw one bunch of dates and one of grapes. He ate until he was satiated and drank the water that was at the table. Thereafter,*

he extended his sacred hands to wash them. Gabriel poured the water, Michael washed them, and Raphael wiped his hands. They then ascended to the Heavens with the leftover food.

After his meal, Muhammad would stand to perform some prayers in gratitude of his Lord. Gabriel reappeared and told him, "The prayers are forbidden upon you at this moment. You must go and be with Khadija, for God has promised Himself that tonight He shall create a virtuous child from your loins."

The Prophet rejoiced and proceeded to the house of Khadija after those forty days of patience in separation. Khadija would narrate this story later in her life.

I was accustomed to living alone during this period, and when it would get dark, I would cover my head, draw the curtains and lock the doors. I would then offer my prayers, turn off the lights and retire for the night. During that night, I was half-awake when the Prophet arrived and softly knocked at the door. I asked, 'Who knocks at the door, for knocking at this door is not lawful for anyone except Muhammad.'

The Prophet of God replied with a sweet and soft voice, 'O Khadija! Open the door, I am Muhammad.' I was overjoyed and opened the door and the Prophet entered therein. It was the custom of the Prophet that whenever he entered the house, he would call for water, perform the ablution, offer two units of prayers, and then he would retire for the evening. But that night, he neither asked for water, nor prayed, but instead, he reclined on the bed with me. He arose from the bed and by God, the Prophet had not yet left me when I felt the light of Fatima in my womb and felt the heaviness of pregnancy within me.

She was conceived of that sacred fruit and divine decree. It is no wonder why from her cradle and to his grave, the Prophet kissed Fatima's hands and smelled her heavenly fragrance, ascending closer and closer to Paradise each time.

CHAPTER 2

THE ORCHARDS OF ABU TALIB

Fatima is the mother of her father.

– The Prophet Muhammad

Though Fatima was born to immaculate parents, the society around her was far from it. Fatima's childhood was marked by the oppression and horrid crimes of the Meccans. As a young girl, she saw her father persecuted, insulted, and abused.

Fatima would accompany her father as a toddler and small child when he went to pray in the House of God. One day, she followed him as he had left early to the mosque to recite the verses of God and immerse himself in prayer before the house that his forefathers Abraham and Ismail built many years before his time. The young Fatima entered the mosque looking for her father. She spotted the Messenger of God reciting the Holy Quran as he sat in the Hijr of Ismail near the Kaaba. She smiled and began walking towards him to join her father in worship.

Still at a distance, Fatima watched some of the Meccans close in on the Prophet. She apparently was not the only one watching him. As the Prophet brought his body to the ground in prostration, the group of Meccans grabbed bags of rubbish and dumped them on the back of the Prophet. Covering him with filth as he was indulged in worship, they laughed and dispersed.

The young Fatima rushed to her father as tears ran down her cheeks. Fatima wiped off the rubbish from her father's back and shoulders and removed what she could off his clothes. She was not scared or anxious of the harm those men could have brought her as a defenseless child. Her only worry was for her father, the Prophet, and how men had the audacity to mistreat him when his only sin was prostrating before the One. The care Fatima showed her father was that of a mother for her child. That care could move mountains, and in Muhammad's eyes it did.

Muhammad embraced his daughter Fatima who continued to wipe the rubbish off his clothes as he finished his prayers. He held her beautiful little face in his rugged hands that had shown the wear of an honest living and laboring over the years in service of his fellow man. And yet, those hands had the softest touch for his Fatima. "She is the mother of her father," he would say about his blessed daughter.

With all the hurt and humiliation Muhammad faced in Mecca, having Khadija and his daughter Fatima made all the difference. This was not the only incident of harassment and persecution Muhammad faced, and it did not stop him. Muhammad and his followers were consistently harassed and attacked by the pagans of Mecca. He came with a way of life that threatened their status quo of unjust economic enrichment that they simply could not tolerate.

The Meccans were determined to be rid of Muhammad and his followers. So, the persecution only got worse. It was so bad that Muhammad was forced to take refuge in the orchards of Abu Talib, away from the sights of the Meccans and away from the people.

The Prophet's family and the rest of Banu Hashem joined him in this sanctuary for the safety of the women and children. Still, they continued to live in fear and apprehension as they did not know if and when the Meccans would find them and attack. Every night they went to bed with the thought that tonight may be their last. They were terrorized by the pledge of the Meccans to cut them off. The chiefs of Quraysh boycotted Banu Hashem and ordered economic sanctions that crippled them to their knees. But it is at your knees that you are in the best position to kneel before your Lord and pray, for He is the one who answers and saves.

Hunger began for Fatima when she was only two years old. Banu Hashem continued to face hard times with the sanctions, which lasted for over three years. In those three years, Fatima saw the calamities at hand. She grew up knowing what it meant to sacrifice for your beliefs and to remain patient against all the odds. It was as if these were the training grounds that built the character she would have in the years ahead of her, ones that would require even greater sacrifice and patience.

Still, what patience can be had by children who suffered from hunger for days at a time? What was the sin of these children who cried in the middle of the night unable to sleep because of the emptiness that ruled their little stomachs? They had no sin.

Their cries would be heard by the people of Mecca and echo into the night. The Meccan antagonists smiled smugly, while the increasing number of sympathizers grew in sorrow.

What brought Fatima ease as a young child who cared for her father more than the entire world was the sight of Abu Talib at his side. She loved Abu Talib, her great uncle. Fatima admired his unwavering support to her father. His bravery and courage were seen at every situation she witnessed. She watched as Abu Talib and Hamza stood tall and proud as they walked behind the Messenger of God toward the House of God in Mecca. They came to announce to all those present that they were followers and supporters of Muhammad.

Fatima saw them as warriors with sword and shield standing guard, protecting their commander in a position, forewarning to the impending enemy and the danger ahead. To fortify the guard around the Messenger of God before the enemy Meccans, Abu Talib surrounded the Prophet with his own men.

The young Fatima watched as Abu Talib made his declaration of faith to all the Meccans crystal clear. He stood before the crowds that had gathered and announced his position before them.

"You have come to prevent the Messenger, the Messenger of the King... Now I am here, and I will protect the Messenger of the King," Abu Talib said as he looked into their eyes with a fierceness of conviction in the King of Kings.

Fatima closely watched from the examples around her – her father, mother, and great uncle – and found that true greatness comes with great sacrifice. She saw that firsthand from her family. With Abu Talib's support of his nephew Muhammad, the Prophet continued to be challenged in his message, and with Khadija by his side as his full support and backbone. Fatima saw in her mother the perfect exemplar of what it means to be a woman. She was her husband's support system, she was his rock. Khadija was there for him in everything – emotionally, financially, and spiritually. Her mind, body and spirit were fully vested in support of his mission and work. Still, Khadija was her own person.

The successes she had amassed as a businesswoman could not be enumerated. By far, Khadija was one of the wealthiest, most intelligent, and most successful merchants of Arabia. But all that wealth and all that success kneeled before her belief and commitment to the Messenger of God, her husband. It was in the arms of such a woman that the Lady of Light would grow and glimmer. But the light of Fatima's eyes would be taken from her while she was just a child. Khadija would return to her Lord.

Khadija had wealth that could fill the valleys of Mecca far and wide, but she had not used it for herself. If she had, she probably would have lived for much longer and enjoyed the many comforts of life for many more years to come. But the worldly life was nothing more than a mirage to her. Her money was only a tool in the way of God, and that is how she used it.

She sacrificed all her wealth to support Islam and the Muslims during the three-year boycott they endured. She bought Muslim slaves from the Meccan markets and gave them their freedom. She assisted families in getting them back on their feet and providing for their children. Khadija was the welfare system of the new Muslim community.

She went hungry, so long as the children ate. She went cold, so long as the women were clothed with warmth. She went thirsty, so long as the families drank. She grew tired and did not bat an eyelash, so long as her people found comfort. Throughout the adversities, she smiled. She smiled just like Muhammad smiled. She followed his footsteps and, in his absence, led the way. She was his everything. She was Khadija.

On her deathbed, Khadija could not rid herself of the agony of separation from her flower Fatima. She knew how devastated Fatima would be by her death, and it pained her. Khadija believed whole heartedly in the plan of God and embraced her destiny. As the clouds of death hovered over her, her beloved Muhammad came to her bedside.

"Though I say this with pain seeing you like this, when you see your sisters do send them greetings."

Khadija replied, "And what sisters do you mean O' Messenger of God?"

"Mariam bint Imran, Kulthum the sister of Moses, and Asia the wife of Pharaoh."

"My pleasure, O' Messenger of God," she smiled at her beloved.

The Prophet was ordered by God to tell Khadija of her abode in paradise. He held her, tears filling his eyes and his heart aching for the coming separation, yet trying to console her. "A castle built of pearls, a home with no noise or remanences of bickering and discord, which will be yours in paradise."

For a few moments, the Prophet left the room. Asma bint Umays came to the bedside of Khadija who began crying and shaking. Trying to console her and calm her down Asma told her not to cry.

"How do you cry, when you are the Lady of all Ladies? And when you are the wife of the Prophet? And when you have been promised Paradise by the Prophet himself?"

Khadija wiped away her tears with her shaking hands and looked at Asma. "I do not cry for myself," she said. "Every young lady comes to the night of her wedding, having her mother next to her for whatever she needs. I fear that my Fatima will not have anyone by her side on her day."

Asma took Khadija's hand and came in closer.

"I promise you, my Lady Khadija, if God gives me life until then, I will be in your place for our Fatima. Don't you worry," Asma assured Khadija.

Khadija's heart found some ease and her soul was ready to depart. At Khadija's death, Muhammad's heart was crushed. He lost his beloved wife who believed in him before anyone did. Khadija was the first Muslim and follower of Muhammad. She was more than any man could ask for or expect. Not only was she the most loving, doting, and caring partner and companion, but she sacrificed alongside the Prophet to spread his message and protect it.

It was the wealth of Khadija, of which she spent willingly and happily, that provided the infrastructure of the Muslim community and supported its growth. If it were not for the wealth of Khadija, Islam would not be. She gave everything that was hers for her belief in her beloved, and ultimately for her unmatched conviction in God.

Khadija would be buried in the Mua'allat Cemetery of Al-Hujun in Mecca. As the Prophet went into her grave to prepare it for her final resting, young Fatima followed him.

"O' Messenger of God, where is my mother?"

The Prophet held back his tears and could not answer her. Fatima continued to circle around him, gently tugging at his thobe, repeating her question quietly.

"Where is my mother?"

In those moments, Angel Gabriel descended upon the Prophet.

> Your Lord commands you to relay peace to Fatima and to tell her, 'Your mother is in a castle made of pearls, its steps are of gold and its pillars are made from red rubies. She is amongst Asia the wife of Pharaoh and Mariam bint Imran.

So, the Prophet obliged and told her those exact words.

At her young age, Fatima replied with such simple eloquence, "Allah is peace, from Him is peace, and to Him peace shall return."

With no money left to purchase a shroud to bury his Khadija in, the Prophet wrapped and buried Khadija in his cloak. Fatima and Muhammad stood at her grave, embracing each other in the love of the daughter of Khuwaylid. What brought further injury to these blessed hearts was that only a month later, Abu Talib passed away. Abu Talib was not only the Prophet's beloved uncle, he was one of his greatest and most important supporters in his mission. For many years, the only thing that came between the Meccans and killing Muhammad was the presence of Abu Talib. But now he was gone.

That year would become known as "The Year of Sorrow", as it devastated the Prophet and changed the course of history. With both Khadija and Abu Talib gone, Mecca was no longer a possibility for Muhammad. Migration was destiny.

CHAPTER 3

A CITY TO CALL HOME

I have not seen anyone more like the Messenger of God in virtue, guidance and speech than Fatima, his daughter…

– Aisha bint Abu Bakr

The threat on the Prophet's life would only become more imminent. The Meccans did not care for the loss of his dearest family members. They rejoiced at the death of Abu Talib and had no sympathy for the loss of Muhammad's wife Khadija. The Prophet knew that the Meccans had no bounds and would do anything to be rid of him, once and for all.

Lo and behold, the Chiefs of Quraysh devised a plan to assassinate Muhammad in his home. They wished to kill him in the late hours before dawn, where he lay asleep at night. Though Abu Talib was no longer alive to protect Muhammad, he was still confident in God's plan. For Muhammad had his Lord to protect him, and his Lord would give him Ali ibn Abi Talib.

When the Holy Prophet made his miraculous escape to Yathrib, he left Fatima behind, but, of course, she was not left alone. The Prophet entrusted Fatima to his greatest trustee – Ali. In fact, Muhammad had given his cousin Ali all the responsibilities he had in Mecca upon his departure. The most important of them all, to care for Fatima's wellbeing and ensure she was brought to Yathrib safe and sound.

Yathrib would be renamed "Medina", and Medina would be what they called home. Still, before arriving in their new home, they would face challenges along the way. After carrying out the other responsibilities the Prophet tasked him with, such as fulfilling some outstanding debts and returning trusts to particular individuals, Ali was ready to make his journey to Medina. Entrusted to him were the three Fatimas: his mother Fatima bint Asad, his cousin Fatima bint Al-Zubayr, and the daughter of the Prophet Fatima bint Muhammad.

The women's veils were worn long and wide, protecting them from the harsh desert wind, as well as the harsh Bedouin eyes. They rode upon the camels while Ali walked on foot. His feet blistered and bloodied by the scorching ground, but he paid it no attention. His mission was clear, and the time was near. He would reach his destination and deliver the trust to his master Muhammad. Ali was barely 21 years old in those days.

On the road, Ali and the women he escorted were quickly surrounded by a band of horsemen outside of Medina. The horsemen encircled the Prophet's family with a devious intent. Their faces were covered as they rode their horses, trotting around Ali and the women. The women came in closer, clenching on to one another.

"Stop your men," Ali stood before the horsemen. "Be with ease and let us be."

"Calm down," Ibn Utba told his men. "Let us hear what Ali has to say," he removed the veil that covered his face.

"You know that I am a man of virtue, and I know that you are virtuous men as well. We are resolved on reaching our destination. Ask and request what you may without malice," Ali said with a diplomatic firmness that was unique to the young warrior.

"Where are you going with these Hashimite women? Is it not unfortunate that you are to leave Mecca in such a way?" Ibn Utba asked as he circulated Ali with his men.

"The Meccans know the status and value of Muhammad's family very well. O' Ali, go back with these women now without any bickering!"

Ibn Utba turned red in the face and came closer to Ali.

"I'll say it once more Ibn Utba. We are headed to Yathrib and we will not change our course," Ali said looking Ibn Utba straight in his eyes.

Ibn Utba turned for a moment checking his horsemen.

"And you know your men are no match for me," Ali promised.

"Do you realize what you said?" Ibn Utba exclaimed.

"Yes."

"You said you were going to Yathrib," Ibn Utba added.

"Yes, I did," Ali replied simply.

"And that you will not change your course no matter what?!"

"That is what I said," Ali responded calmly.

"I see that you have here Fatima bint Al-Zubayr," Ibn Utba pointed at one of the women. "And this is Fatima bint Asad, your mother. Here also you have Fatima bint Muhammad."

Standing tall as Ibn Utba trotted around stating the obvious, Ali loosely grabbed the handle of his sheathed sword. He was ready at any moment.

"These horsemen and I, who are the greatest of Mecca's warriors, have come here only to bring you back! Either you come back with us on your feet or without your heads! The choice is yours."

Ali did not move an inch. He stood between Ibn Utba and the women he swore to protect. He looked Ibn Utba dead in the eyes and did not say a word.

"Men! Take the women and I will take care of this one myself!"

Ibn Utba pulled his sword on Ali and swung with all his might. Ali quickly maneuvered around him, his sword still in its sheath, and kicked him to the ground.

"If any of you has the nerve to do anything foolish, I promise none of you will be left alive." Ali unsheathed his sword and raised it to the sky as it glistened and glimmered against the desert's sun.

The soldiers stood in their tracks and did not dare to come near the women. A mix of fear and awe overcame them as they gazed at the grandeur of the young warrior. Ali grabbed Ibn

Utba, who laid startled on the ground below. Holding him by the collar and with his sword to his neck, Ali made it clear to Ibn Utba.

"I am not bloodthirsty. Go and tell the Meccans that Ali is with Muhammad in peace and war," Ali said.

Ibn Utba still disoriented could not gather words as he did so plentifully moments ago.

"Now go!"

Ali released him and Ibn Utba hurried off with his horsemen back to Mecca. Lady Fatima, as the other Fatimas, saw the bravery and valor of Ali. She would never forget that day in which he not only saved their lives, but he honored the name of her father and their Prophet.

Fatima would grow up in the arms of the City of Knowledge that was her father Muhammad. He sat down with her daily, revealing the verses of God to her and explaining their meanings. He guided her on matters of life and spoke to her as his student and disciple. Fatima saw in his words the true meaning of life and salvation. Sitting with her one day, the Prophet advised Fatima.

"He whose neighbor is not safe from his harms is not from the believers. He who believes in God and in the afterlife, would not harm his neighbor. He who believes in God and in the afterlife, should say good or otherwise keep silent. God loves a good, patient, ascetic one, and abhors an indecent, stingy, importunate one. Coyness is from faith, and faith is in Paradise. Indecency is from obscenity, and obscenity is in Hellfire…".

The Prophet would take his daughter with him to the mosque for worship. As they entered, he told his beloved, "Fatima, when we enter the mosque say, 'O God, forgive me my sins and open to me the doors of Your mercy...'".

They would continue on into the House of God and worship Him, and Him alone. Of the supplications the Prophet taught his daughter, he advised her with the following prayer to God.

O' You the knowing of the unseen and the hidden secrets, the obeyed, the knower – O' God, O' God, O' God – the defeater of the parties in aid of Muhammad, the planner against the Pharaoh for Moses, the saver of Jesus from the hands of the unjust, the rescuer of Noah's people from the flood, the merciful to Your servant Jacob, the reliever of Job's distress, the saver of Jonah from darkness, the doer of every good, the guide to every good, the leader to every good, the enjoiner on every good, the creator of every good, the qualified for good... You are God. I have come to You for what You know, and You are the knower of the unseen. I ask you to have blessing on Muhammad and the progeny of Muhammad.

When they left the mosque, Fatima would look to her father awaiting how else she should invoke her Lord. The Prophet turned to his daughter and said, "And as you leave the mosque say, 'O God, forgive me my sins and open to me the doors of Your favor...'"

From these prayers and supplications, lessons and values, Fatima watched her father and became his shadow. She was very similar to him in her character, personality, speech, and even the way she walked.

"Whenever I saw Fatima walk, I remembered the Messenger of God. She inclined to the right one time and then to the left another," Jabir ibn Abdillah Al-Ansary, one of the close companions of the Prophet, would say.

It was a reality that virtually no one could deny. Fatima was the impeccable reflection of God's Prophet. Be it from near or far, people saw this perfectly. Aisha, would observe the relationship between Fatima and the Prophet. She would describe,

> I have not seen anyone more like the Messenger of God in virtue, guidance, and speech than Fatima his daughter. When she came to the Messenger of God, he got up and kissed her, and seated her in his place. When the Messenger of God came to her, she got up and kissed him, and seated him in her place.

Returning from one of his battles, the Prophet came to the House of Fatima. That was always his first destination upon returning home. Welcoming her father, Fatima touched his blessed face and kissed his eyes. She cried as she embraced him.

"My dear Fatima, why are you crying?" the Prophet asked her worriedly.

"I see that you have turned pale," she replied with tears in her eyes.

The Prophet held her tight and calmed her down. He looked at his daughter with his serene smile and reassured her.

"O' Fatima, God the Almighty has delegated your father with a mission that no house on the face of the Earth remains until it is entered with glory or with spite. It will reach wherever night falls." Glory is for those who believe in Him and spite is for those who deny God and fight Him.

Fatima smiled back at her father and thanked him as the 'Messenger of God.' She often addressed him as such, especially after the revelation of the verse: "Make not the calling of the messenger among you as your calling one another." (24:63).

The Prophet embraced his daughter again and told her,

O' Fatima, the verse was not revealed about you, your family, or your progeny. You are from me and I am from you. It was revealed about the harsh and rude people of Quraysh, the people of lavishness and haughtiness. You call me, 'father'. That is more refreshing to my heart and more pleasing to the Lord.

"Father", a word that no one could say to the Prophet but Fatima. And O how he loved to hear her say that word to him. It brought the greatest joy to his heart and was most pleasing to his Lord.

They spent their days and nights in such a manner. Enjoying each other's blessed company, sharing reflections of the divine, and giving all they had to better the lives of others.

Fatima was the mirrored image of her father, as a child and then as a young lady. Prophet Muhammad watched her grow and with every day saw her look more and more like her mother Khadija. He smiled and teared at the same time. She was growing up so quickly.

What a beautiful sight to see his young flower grow with such spiritual and intellectual elegance and distinction. It was almost as if she was not from this worldly abode. Fatima manifested the generosity of her mother and the valor of her father. She lived with the kindness of Muhammad and the selflessness of Khadija. She embodied the brilliance of her mother and the excellence of her father. She was Khadija and Muhammad in one. But as she grew and her perfection was ever so brilliant, Muhammad contemplated a question. Who could possibly be a match for his daughter, the Lady of Light?

CHAPTER 4

A MATCH MADE IN HEAVEN

If God had not created Ali ibn Abi Talib, there would be no match for my Fatima.

– The Prophet Muhammad

As a young lady, Fatima had scores of suitors come to the Prophet's door asking for her hand in marriage. To be the son-in-law of the Messenger of God and the husband of his only daughter was no ordinary honor. Thus, practically every man of status or confidence, regardless of whether it was founded, asked for Fatima's hand. One after another, they were denied. There was simply no match for Fatima amongst those that presented themselves. There was only one, and he had not yet come.

Finally, the day would arrive that Ali ibn Abi Talib would walk to the house of his cousin, his brother Muhammad, and ask for Fatima's hand. That was the day the Prophet celebrated like no other day, and his heart filled with joy. Lady Fatima would be wed to Ali, a divine match written in the Heavens. Ali was the last person to ask for Fatima's hand, when dozens had gone before him and were turned away. It was not only Fatima's choice to marry Ali, but in the Prophet's eyes there was simply no one in creation that would be a better partner.

"If God had not created Ali ibn Abi Talib, there would be no match for my Fatima," the Prophet would say happily after Fatima bashfully consented to Ali's proposal.

Those who proposed to Fatima had promised wealth and worldly possessions that could fill the deserts of Arabia. It was of no interest to Fatima or the Prophet. Abdulrahman ibn Awf would be one of the many to ask for Fatima's hand. He knocked on the door of the Prophet and walked in with a false sense of confidence.

As he sat with the Messenger of God, he brought forth the conversation. In his proposal, he described to the Prophet what he would give for Fatima's hand in marriage.

"If you give Fatima to me in marriage, I will give her a dowry of one hundred camels with chests of precious stones from Egypt along with ten thousand dinars."

Hearing this, the Prophet flushed in the face.

"Do you think that I am a servant of wealth that you express pride in the dowry which you want to give to marry my daughter?"

The Prophet looked away from him and told him to leave.

For Fatima's dowry, the Prophet spoke in part to his daughter and reassured her of what value her marriage gift would be.

"If there was another person better than Ali in my family, I would have married you to him… I did not marry you to Ali except that I consider him to be your pristine match… As for your dowry, it will be a fifth of this world for eternity."

Fatima rejoiced with her father's kindness and saw only goodness in what was to come of her marriage. Ali did not have wealth or material possession, in fact that was one of the reasons for his initial hesitation in asking for Fatima's hand. Ali saw that Fatima deserved the whole world and everything in it, but he did not own anything to offer her. In his bashful conversation with his cousin, Ali expressed his embarrassment.

The Prophet said, "Ali what do you own so that you may give something to Fatima as a dowry?"

Ali was the bravest warrior that Islam, let alone the entire world, had seen. All he had were those things that a warrior should have for battle – a sword to fight with, a shield to protect his body, and a horse to ride into battle.

"As for your horse, you need it, and as for your sword, you cannot do without it. But as for your shield, you can sell that," the Prophet told his cousin Ali.

Ali would go to the market and sell his shield, the amount of which came to be four hundred and eighty dirhams. He came back to the Prophet with the dirhams knotted in by the end of his shirt. "When I sold the shield and brought the money to the Prophet, he did not ask me how much it was, nor did I tell him," Ali would say.

The Prophet took a handful of the money and gave it to his companion, Bilal al-Habashi. "Buy some perfume for Fatima from this," he instructed Bilal. Then he took two handfuls from the dirhams and handed it to Salman and Um Salama. The Prophet instructed them as follows.

"From this amount, buy whatever is suitable for Fatima with regards to household necessities."

They went to the market and bought Fatima all they could with that amount. They would go on to get Fatima a dress worth seven dirhams, a shawl worth four dirhams, a black gown from the cloth of Khaybar, a mattress filled with the leaves of a palm tree, four pillows of tanned hide made in Taif filled with dry grass, two Egyptian quilts, one stuffed with wool and the other with the leaves of a palm tree, a handmill to grind wheat, a waterskin specially made to cool water, a straw mat stitched in the Bahraini town of Hajar, a copper tub, a clay bowl, an earthen pitcher that was colored from inside, a green clay ewer, and a few cups made of clay.

And that would be what filled the new house of Fatima – one outfit, pillows filled with leaves, and pottery. Though by any standards this was ascetic, simple, and minimal; to the House of the Prophet, it was perfect.

"Blessed are the people of a house whose vessels are mostly of pottery," the Prophet said and smiled.

The house of Fatima may seem peculiar in its simplicity to the reader, but it should be to no surprise. Even the people of her time were shocked by how humble, modest, and simple she lived.

"How is it that Fatima, the daughter of Muhammad, lives this way?" people would ask dumbfounded as to austerity of her situation. The Prophet would smile at the question and say, "Verily my daughter is among the foremost ones in the eyes of God."

The engagement was about a month long and Ali waited patiently. He was overjoyed to have Fatima as his wife, partner, and the love of his heart. But a month could also be a long time indeed.

"One month passed after these events, I prayed along with the Prophet of God and went to my house, but I did not utter a word to him regarding the actual marriage," Imam Ali would say.

At that time, some of the wives of the Prophet came to Ali and asked him.

"Should we speak to the Prophet on your behalf to send Fatima to your house?"

"Could you speak to him?" Ali asked bashfully.

The women readily went to the Prophet and sat before him. Amongst them, Um Ayman, addressed the Holy Prophet with a few words.

"O Prophet of God, I have come to you regarding a matter that if Khadija had been alive, she would have been delighted to hear... Ali would like to take his wife to his home. Let Fatima be delighted by the glance of her husband and so too will we be delighted."

The Prophet replied to Um Aymen's request with a question.

"Why does Ali himself not speak to me regarding this matter? I expect that he should precede you."

"O Prophet of God, modesty refrains me from speaking to you regarding this matter," Ali replied to his father-in-law in humility.

Content with Ali's response, the Prophet looked around and asked, "Who is present here?"

Um Salama replied, "I am at your service."

"Prepare a room from among the adjacent rooms for my daughter Fatima and my cousin Ali."

"Which room would you like us to prepare?" Um Salama asked.

The Prophet replied, "Your room."

The doting father instructed his wives to care for Fatima, to adorn her, and treat her as the royalty she was. They surrounded her and were at her service. The heavenly maiden had no requests, but the women were ready to fulfill even those that were unsaid.

Um Salama came to Fatima with a heart ready to serve. She asked, "Do you have perfume?"

"Yes," Fatima replied simply.

Fatima reached for the perfume and sprinkled droplets of it in Um Salama's palm. She raised her hand to smell the scent and could not compare it to anything she had smelled before.

"Where did you get this perfume from?" Um Salama asked with intrigue.

Fatima would tell her the story of the heavenly perfume.

"One day, Dihyah al-Kalbi came with the Prophet and my father told me, 'O Fatima, bring a mat for your uncle.' I brought a mat and spread it on the floor, and they sat upon it. When they stood up, something scattered upon the floor from his clothes. My father told me, 'Gather this.' Ali then asked the Prophet as to what it was that we were gathering. The Prophet replied, 'This is amber that has fallen from the wings of Gabriel.'"

Later, the Prophet would come to Ali and tell him to prepare a dinner for the family. As with anything Muhammad instructed his cousin, Ali was up for the task.

"Prepare food for your relatives," the Prophet said. "The meat and bread will be arranged by us, while you take care of the oil and dates."

Ali went on his way to buy the oil and dates as he was told. He hurried back as not to delay and presented the dates and oil before his cousin. The Prophet rolled up his sleeves and mixed the dates in the oil. He also had sent for a large meaty sheep and heaves of bread with it.

"You may invite anyone you desire," the Prophet told his cousin Ali with a smile.

Ali smiled back and made his way to the Mosque. There he saw scores of companions. Ali could not bear the thought of some being invited while others are left out or neglected. He decided that he would invite them all. With his welcoming voice, Ali called out to the crowd of companions.

"You are all invited to a dinner for the betrothal of Fatima!"

It was the most beautiful invitation they could have received. Hearing this, they all came. Every single one of the men attended. They were many, possibly a little too many.

"I was embarrassed due to the large number of men and the small quantity of food," Ali would later narrate in his life.

When the Prophet perceived his embarrassment, he looked at Ali with a twinkle in his eyes and reassured him.

"I will pray to my Lord to grant abundance to this food."

The simple dinner turned to a feast and hundreds of people took part in the feast. All who came ate and were filled to the brim, but the food did not seem to finish. People were happy and the air filled with joy and laughter. The Prophet's smile was contagious. He beamed and they all smiled back. He called for additional bowls to fill with some more food. The Prophet sent the bowls of food to his wives. He then took another bowl, filling it with food as well, and said, "This one is for Fatima and her husband."

That is how he was to Fatima. He always thought of her, even when she was already cared for. She was the apple of his eye and the light of his heart. He loved her more than the world and everything in it.

Three days passed after Fatima moved into the house of Ali, and the Prophet did not visit them. On Wednesday morning, he paid them a visit while Asma bint Umays, the Prophet's wife, was found present there. Wondering why she was at their home, the Prophet took her to the side to speak to her.

"Why have you come here when the man (Ali) is here?"

"May my parents be your ransom! When a woman goes to her husband's home and passes the first days of her marriage, she needs another woman who can attend to her needs, thus I have come here," Asma replied to the Prophet bashfully.

Filled with a heart of awe and joy, the Prophet answered, "O Asma! May God fulfill your desires of this world as well as the next."

Days after, the Prophet would come knocking on the door of the newlyweds. As soon as Ali heard the knock, followed by the Prophet's voice, he was rejoiced. To be visited by his cousin and brother was an honor worthy of celebration each and every time.

"O Prophet of God, please enter, glad tidings to the ones hosting you and peace be upon the one who comes."

The Prophet entered with his radiating smile and greeted Fatima and Ali. Fatima sat by his side and he embraced her as he always had. He then turned to her after some moments and said,

"O Fatima, go and bring me some water my dear."

Fatima got up and filled a cup with water and brought it to him. The Prophet took the water and blessed it with his touch.

"Face me my dear," he said.

Fatima directed herself to her father Muhammad.

Facing him, he then sprinkled some water upon her, in between her shoulders where lay her impeccable heart. The Prophet then turned to the Heavens and prayed to God.

"O Lord! This is my daughter, the most beloved to me from any other creation. And O Lord, this is Ali, my brother and the most beloved to me, more than any other creation. O Lord! Make him Your friend and aide and make his household a means of prosperity for him."

The Holy Prophet would then look towards Ali.

"Be with your wife, Ali, may God make her a means of abundance for you, and may the mercy and blessings of God be upon you, the One who is worthy of praise, exaltation and commendation."

When winter came, Fatima and Ali would often cover themselves together underneath a heavy large blanket. The Prophet knocked on their door as he always had. Wanting to answer the door, Ali and Fatima would begin to come out from under the blanket. The Prophet would, however, call out to them to remain.

"By the right that I hold upon you, stay put until I come to you," he said. They welcomed him as they always had, and he joined them to cover from the blistering cold of the desert winter nights.

"Bring me a bowl of water," he told Ali.

Ali went to the kitchen and brought him the bowl. The Prophet would blow on the water three times reciting verses from the Holy Quran.

"Drink this water and leave some," he said to Ali. Ali did as the Prophet asked. Muhammad then carried on, sprinkling the remaining on Ali's head and chest praying, "May God keep every uncleanliness away from you O Ali and purify you a thorough purification."

Ali was showered with the Prophet's blessing. He smiled contentedly as he enjoyed Heaven's grace.

Then the Prophet asked for another bowl of water. Ali fetched yet another for his cousin. Again, he recited special verses of God's revelation upon it and blew on the water three times. The Prophet then turned to his daughter Fatima who was watching as Ali performed the Prophet's requested tasks.

"Drink this water and leave some," he said to his daughter.

Fatima graciously drank the prophetic water and handed the bowl back to her father. The Prophet sprinkled the remaining water upon her head and chest like he did moments ago for Ali and said the same prayer. He then asked Ali to give him and Fatima a few moments to speak privately.

"My dear daughter, how are you?" The Prophet asked Fatima as he held her hand.

"How do you find your husband?" he followed.

"Dear father, I found my husband to be the absolute best," Fatima paused.

The Prophet waited for her to continue.

"However, a group of Qurayshi women visited me and said that my father had married me to an indigent man."

The Prophet looked at Fatima and said,

My daughter, neither is your father indigent nor is your husband! God has given me authority upon all the gold and silver treasures of this Earth, but I have preferred the reward of my Lord over it all. My dear daughter, if you know what your father knows, the world would seem wretched in your eyes. I swear by God, that I have not been stingy with regards to your wellbeing. Your husband is the foremost in Islam, the most knowledgeable among any and all, and the most forbearing. O my daughter! God exclusively beheld the Earth and chose two men from among all – one he made your father and the other your husband. O my daughter! Your husband is a virtuous husband. Obey him in all matters."

The Prophet then called Ali back into the room.

"Yes, O Messenger of God?" Ali responded as he walked in the room.

"Enter your home and treat your wife with love and kindness, for Fatima is a piece of me and whoever hurts her, hurts me, and whoever pleases her, pleases me. I offer you to God and may He be your Protector," the Prophet said.

History would tell of Ali's reflections on those days. He would tell his family and close companions of his deep love and adoration for his beloved Fatima. He said, "I swear by God, I never made her angry nor forced her to do anything until God, the Mighty, the Sublime, took away her soul. She never made me uneasy, nor did she ever disobey me, and whenever I looked at her, all of my grief and sorrow vanished away."

CHAPTER 5

OURS AND YOURS

Come! Let us call our sons and your sons, our women and your women, our souls and your souls, then let us pray earnestly, and call down Allah's curse upon the liars.

– Holy Quran 3:61

As Lady Fatima endured the sight of her father being humiliated and harassed by the pagans of Quraysh, she also saw his glorious victories and the triumph of their faith. Fatima watched as Islam would grow and people flocked to the religion. She stood by the side of her husband Ali and her father Muhammad as they engaged in battle after battle, defending the oppressed and persecuted. She saw time after time, how truth prevailed, and how falsehood was exposed. It was not a sentiment or a slogan, it was what they lived and breathed. It was in the water they drank and the stale bread they ate.

It was this heritage that Fatima passed down to her blessed children, the Princes of Banu Hashem, Hasan and Husayn, and her two daughters Zainab and Umme Kulthoom. Lady Fatima raised her children on this glorious path of truth. They would grow to carry her legacy and honor the purpose of their existence in every breath they took. No matter how young they were or what they were doing, they exemplified that beautiful existence that Fatima radiated. Like the sun gives light to its moon, Fatima blessed her beloved children with her aura.

Lady Fatima raised her two sons as the princes they were meant to be – the next two purified and infallible Imams of the people, and the leaders of the youth of paradise. Once, upon visiting the Prophet, she said, "O Father, these are your two sons. Please, gift them a part of your nobility and morals to leave with them."

With adoring eyes, the Prophet responded, "As for Al-Hasan, he shall have my gravity and glory, and as for Al-Husayn, he shall have my courage and generosity."

The Prophet's family were right by his side, both when he was challenged by oppressors, and when he invited people to his path. The call he made to the Christians of Najran was an example of such a time, and against the backdrop of history stands to be one of the most brilliant highlights in the life of Lady Fatima.

After the Prophet returned and conquered Mecca ten years after his migration, his invitations to neighboring cities and tribes increased. People had come into the fold of Islam and the religion began spreading across the region. The people saw in Islam, and its prophet, protection, security, and salvation. Prophet Muhammad sent emissaries and ambassadors to towns across Arabia inviting them to Islam and declaring peace with all those who wished to live in amity and harmony. One of the groups that received such an invitation were the Christians of Najran.

There were approximately forty-thousand people living in the province called Najran. The mountainous region in the northern parts of Yemen was home to about seventy smaller towns in which those thousands lived. Historically, they were pagans just like their Arab neighbors to the north; however, they came to worship God through Christianity after the mission of a priest by the name of Phemion. Through his work, the area almost entirely converted to Christianity and Najran was soon enough a focal point for Christians of the region. Just like they turned from paganism to Christianity, many of the Arabs to the north turned from idol-worship to the religion of Muhammad – Islam.

In his letter to the people of Najran, Prophet Muhammad addressed Grand Bishop Abu Al-Harith ibn 'Alqama. Ibn 'Alqama was designated as the Roman Church's official representative and authority in Arabia. The Prophet invited him and his people to the religion of Islam. In the invitation, the Prophet ensured protection to their people by the Muslims, regardless if they accept his faith or not. The difference was that if they came under the fold of Islam, they would be held to the obligations of the religion and what it mandated of alms and taxes. If they continued in their own faith, they would be exposed to the Jizya tax which would compensate for what they would otherwise be contributing to the state as Muslims.

The leadership at Najran deliberated the matter after receiving Muhammad's letter. They finally decided that they would send a delegation to Medina to engage in a dialogue with Muhammad and his followers. The group was led by their bishop,

Abu Al-Harith, and chief strategist, Al-'Aqib. After days of travel, they finally reached Medina.

Their entrance into the city was an extravagant one. Their robes of silk trailed behind them, and precious stones glimmered on the ring settings around their stout fingers. Gold chains and bracelets hung around their necks and dressed their wrists. Some of the people of Medina gazed at them in awe, enthralled by their pomp and lavishness. It was as if emperors had arrived for a grand event and awaited to be announced. Their reputation preceded them, both men being known for their esteem and stature in the Roman Church, as well as for their astuteness and intelligence.

The delegation finally entered the Prophet's Mosque, where he was awaiting his guests. Upon their entrance, the Prophet was taken aback and was not shy to react to the sight before him. They waited to be greeted and welcomed by the Prophet, but he paid them no attention.

He had turned his face away and tended to the humble men and women that had asked for his guidance and help nearly every day. To thousands, Muhammad was not only a messenger and prophet. He was a support system for the oppressed, and a leader and head of state for the many who followed him.

The Najran delegation was confused and deflated. People paid no more attention to their flashy presence, and so they left the Mosque. Outside, they met with Abulrahman ibn Awf and Uthman ibn Affan.

"Why were we invited by the Muslims and then treated in such a way?" they asked Uthman.

Uthman replied simply, "It would be best to consult with Ali ibn Abi Talib for this, he would know."

Puzzled and searching for answers, they came before Ali. The delegation complained to Ali of the matter and asked what the reason was for this.

Ali explained that they offended the Prophet in arriving in such a way. They displayed arrogance and conceit by the way they dressed and carried themselves. Muslims do not humble themselves before the arrogant, he explained, but embrace and welcome the humble with warmth and open arms. The men took his words with some pause and reflection. Ali then advised that they change their clothes into something more appropriate and simple, and once they did, the Prophet would gladly welcome them.

They conceded to Ali's instructions and went back to the Prophet of Islam, leaving their pomp at the door. Surely enough, they were welcomed by the Prophet and even more.

They too wanted to pray, and when they came forward for their moments of bowing and kneeling before their Lord, some of the companions of the Prophet were on edge. The Christians rang the handbells and kneeled in prayer in the Prophet's mosque. At the sight of this some of the companions quickly objected.

"O Messenger of God! This in your mosque?" they said with stern eyes.

"Leave them be," the Prophet replied simply.

The companions took a step back. The bishop and his men were left to pray as they did. Moments after finishing their ritual prayer, they came up to the Prophet and greeted him. After a brief exchange of pleasantries, the Christians asked the Prophet straight away.

"To what do you call?"

"To bear witness that there is no God but God and that I am the Messenger of God. That Jesus, peace be upon him, is a created slave and messenger of God, and he used to eat, drink, and relieve himself," the Prophet replied.

They responded, "Then who was his father?"

In these moments, the Archangel Gabriel revealed to the Prophet the verse: "Say to them – what do you say about Adam, was he a created slave of God, who would eat, drink, relieve himself and cohabit?"

Thus, the Prophet used the verse and asked them the divinely worded question.

The Christians replied, "Yes."

"Then who was his father?" the Prophet followed.

Left with no answer, they did not utter a word in response.

Revelation was given again to Muhammad in those moments through the verses:

> Indeed, the case of Jesus with Allah is like the case of Adam: He created him from dust, then said to him,

'Be,' and he was. This is the truth from your Lord, so
do not be among the skeptics. (3:59-60)

Still silent, the Christians continued to listen closely. This
man did not speak out of mere whim or individual cognition, he
spoke from a higher order indeed. Unable to stand amongst the
Muslims in such a way and be defeated by a few words by one
mere man, they broke their silence.

> *Muhammad, you have hosted us in your city gra-*
> *ciously, and we appreciate you for that. However, we*
> *and the people of Najran for the longest time have fol-*
> *lowed the traditions of our forefathers. Christianity is*
> *our religion, and it will stay that way! We cannot be-*
> *lieve that you are the Messenger of God as you say!*

Another one of their men followed with an impassioned
statement:

> *O' Muhammad, leave us the people of Najran alone.*
> *Leave your tradition to yourself and leave our way of*
> *life to ourselves. We see that we are on the righteous*
> *path, not the Islam that you call to!"*

The companions and the Muslims present in the Mosque
grew into an uproar.

"It is okay," the Prophet gestured with his hand and calmed
his people down. The Prophet would rise from his place on the
ground and address those present.

"All that I say is from God. I gave you the proofs and you have not been able to properly respond. To deliver the last of God's evidence upon you, I offer you to the challenge of Al-Mubahala."

The room went silent and eyes turned wide. The priests looked at one another confused.

"Al-Mubahala?" they asked.

He revealed the verse that followed those prior:

> Should anyone argue with you concerning him, after the knowledge that has come to you, say, 'Come! Let us call our sons and your sons, our women and your women, our souls and your souls, then let us pray earnestly, and call down Allah's curse upon the liars.' (3:61)

The priests whispered amongst themselves and then looked back toward Muhammad.

"You have been just," they said, and consented to the great debate that was to come.

"Where will our meeting place be?" they followed.

"Tomorrow morning on the outskirts of the city," the Prophet replied.

They carried around pompously asserting their sure victory over Muhammad for the next day, which angered the Muslims.

"We will surely bring curse upon those who stand against us and our faith! Our years of supplication and worship will descend upon you and your Messenger!" one of the priests insisted.

"How could you have the audacity to utter these words in our presence?!" a companion of the Prophet snapped back.

"Calm my companions, calm. These men are under my protection. I am allowing them to say and do as they please. They are my guests."

Thus, the delegation was hosted graciously by the Muslims in Medina. The Prophet ensured that they would be taken care of as guests of the city. When the group retired to their quarters, their leaders convened to discuss the day ahead of them.

At the outskirts of Medina, scores of Muslims gathered around, along with the priests of Najran.

"What is your name my good man?" one of the priests asked one of the men near them. He stood tall, handsome, and had an appealing aura about him.

"Abu Rafi', the freed slave of Prophet Muhammad," he replied simply.

"I have a question for you if you could answer me," the priest said.

Abu Rafi' responded, "Sure, go ahead."

"If Muhammad was to arrive, from which direction would he come?"

"From the same direction that we all came. From the place that everyone walked through, directly behind this lone palm tree," Abu Rafi' described pointing afar.

A gust of wind passed through, and Muhammad began to appear in the distance.

"Abu Rafi'," the priest began to say as he looked towards Muhammad. "Who are those people that Muhammad walks with as his group for imprecation?"

"To his right is Ali ibn Abi Talib," Abu Rafi started to say.

"Ali?!" the other priest jumped in. "The same Ali from the Battle of the Trenches? The one who killed Amr ibn Wud?"

"He is the same Ali that killed Al-Harith and Marhab at the Gate of Khaybar," the second priest followed. "But who is that woman alongside him?"

"The woman with him is his beloved daughter," Abu Rafi' replied.

"And she is the wife of Ali?"

"Yes. She is Fatima, the Lady of Light, the Leader of the Women of the Worlds."

The priests turned to each other and spoke in private as they continued to gaze upon the Prophet and his family walking towards them in the distance.

"I believe we have miscalculated this one," the first priest told the second.

"What do you mean?" his companion responded.

"Look at that. Muhammad did not come with soldiers and men. He walks the path of God with his family. I am in awe just looking at them... I haven't seen anything like it."

Muhammad walked carrying his grandson Husayn in one arm, and Hasan holding his other hand walking alongside him. Fatima trailed immediately behind her father, while Ali walked behind her. The closer they got to the gathering place, the more nervous the priests became.

As they watched from behind a date tree that they inadvertently stood behind, they were reconsidering the whole ordeal.

"If those blessed hands are raised to the sky, they will make even the tallest mountains tremble! These are the faces that turn to God and if they ask Him any request, He will answer," one priest uttered in disbelief.

He turned to his comrade and ordered him, "Go! Go and stop him from praying against us! If he does, we'll all be damned."

The priest began running towards the Prophet who had sat with his grandsons on his lap. Muhammad had just begun supplicating and telling his grandsons, "My sons, when I pray you say 'Amen.'"

They nodded their heads as they smiled back at their grandfather the Prophet.

"Wait! Muhammad, please wait! Do not curse us! We do not wish to imprecate!" the priest called out as he ran to the Prophet.

He arrived before the Prophet and begged for mercy. The Prophet lowered his hands and Ali, Fatima, and their sons followed. The Household spared the Christians of Najran, just as they did with any who asked for mercy and clemency.

CHAPTER 6

PILLOWS OF LEAVES

Salman, verily my daughter is among the foremost ones in the eyes of God.

– The Prophet Muhammad

The Prophet's smile was shattered by little to nothing. Two verses of revelation took away the Prophet's smile in a profound way, however.

"And verily hell is certainly the promised abode for them all. For in it are seven gates, and for each of those gates will be a separate party of the sinners assigned," was the first verse. Receiving this piece of revelation, the Prophet wept profusely. He cried so much that his companions cried by the mere sight of his weeping. They could not understand why he cried, nor could they ask him while he was in such a state.

Whenever the Prophet saw Fatima, he was immediately delighted. The companions knew this. So, they thought, let them call upon Fatima to come forth, that way the Prophet could be rejoiced. One of the Prophet's dearest companions and closest members to the family would go on to summon Fatima. When he got to the house, he found Fatima inside, grinding barley at the mill and reciting God's heavenly words.

"And what is with God is better and more lasting," she recited.

He informed her of the Prophet's lamentation. Fatima jumped from where she sat and put on a wornout veil covering her from her head and flowing below her ankles. The old veil had twelve different patches. Those patches were made of date palm leaves.

Before they left, Salman would notice Fatima's patched veil. His eyes widened and he was overcome with tears, tears so severe they almost matched the Prophet's.

"O what grief! The daughters of Caesars and Chosroes adorn dresses of brocade and silk, while the daughter of the Prophet wears a wornout and patched veil!"

The prophet and his household would live at the level of the poorest person amongst them in that time, not raising their standard unless all the impoverished had risen in their means of living.

They went to the lamenting prophet, and when they arrive Fatima would ask her father.

"Prophet of God! Salman is surprised at my dress, when by the Lord who has chosen you by truth, five years have passed since we use a sheet made of sheep's hide, we sleep upon it at night, and during the day we turn it and lay leaves for the camels to eat, while our pillow is also made from the leaves of date-palm."

The Prophet turned towards his companion with tears in his eyes and said, "Salman, verily my daughter is among the fore-most ones in the eyes of God."

"Dear father, may I be your ransom… why do you weep?"

The Prophet recited the above verses revealed by the Angel Gabriel. When Fatima heard the name of hell, she fell down prostrating upon the ground and constantly repeated, "Woe, and woe upon those who enter the fire of hell." A dark place far from the Benevolent Lord's love is no place to be.

Upon hearing the verse, Salman said, "I wish I would have been a sheep, my family would have slaughtered me and torn my hide and I would not have heard the name of hell."

The great companion Abuthar, who was also present, said, "I wish my mother was barren and had not given birth to me so that I could not have heard the name of hell."

Another great companions, Miqdad, would follow such lamentation with his own. "I wish I was a bird in the forest, then I would have been free from accounting and not heard the name of hell."

Finally, Imam Ali would say, 'I wish the beasts would tear my flesh and I wish my mother had not borne me so that I would not have heard the name of hell.'

The Prophet placed his blessed hand on his head, his tears relentless. He continued weeping with his own reflection. Fatima would raise her head from prostration upon hearing her father speak.

*O the lengthy journey! And O the insufficient belong-
ings for the journey of the resurrection! The sinners
will go towards the fire and the fire shall turn them
over. They are the sick persons that none visits them,
and the injured ones that none goes to heal their
wounds. They are the imprisoned ones that none goes
to rescue them from the fire, while their food and
drink is from the fire. They shall turn upside down in
the large vessels filled with fire. They adorn cotton
clothes in this world while their dress in hell shall be of
pieces of fire. They embrace their spouses in this
world, while in hell the devils will embrace them.*

With all their glory as the Prophet's Household, they still saw
themselves as forever indebted to the grace of God. They cared
for others, before themselves. They wept for the sinners, because
of the torture they would bring upon themselves. When God's
doors are always open, why would you settle for the curb?

In this beautiful spirit, Fatima would build her home and
raise her children. One starry Thursday night, the young Hasan
decided not to go to sleep. Instead, he would stay awake as long
as his mother Fatima kneeled in prayer. Hasan watched his
blessed mother as she prostrated and kneeled through the night.
From nightfall until dawn, her lips did not stop moving in supplication. But what were the words she uttered; he could not
make out as he observed her at a distance.

The gracefulness of Fatima's psalms was like the moonlight
upon the waters of a crystal lake. As he watched the final moments of her nightlong prayers, Hasan came in closer to his

mother. Fatima delivered her final salutations and turned to see her eldest son nearby.

Fatima would open her arms and greet Hasan with an embrace that comprehended all the love the world could offer. Her smile brightened up their early dawn even more than the rising sun.

"Mother, may I ask you something?"

"Of course, my darling son."

"I've watched you pray the entirety of the night. As I watched and listened, I did not hear you once make a request to God for your own self... why is that mother?"

Fatima smiled at her beloved son and replied as she caressed the side of his limpid face.

"Your neighbor before yourself, my son. Your neighbor before yourself."

Many years later, Lady Fatima's great grandson Imam Ja'far Al-Sadiq was asked a question by one of his companions. "Why was your mother Fatima given the epithet, 'Al-Zahra'?" The Shining One.

"As she stood in her worship, her light shined for the inhabitants of Heaven as stars shone for the inhabitants of Earth," Al-Sadiq replied.

In another gathering Al-Sadiq spoke of his grandmother's epithet of Al-Zahra to a group of his companions. He said,

Fatima is named 'Al-Zahra' because a dome of red rubies has been created by God for her in Paradise. The height of the dome measures a distance equaling one year of travel and is suspended in the air by the power of God, without being held by chains from the Heavens so as to take care of it, nor is it supported by pillars on the Earth so as to be attached to it. It is suspended in between the Heavens and the Earth. The dome contains ten thousand doors, and on each door, one thousand angels stand on guard. The dwellers of Paradise will behold the dome just as you see the shining stars on the skies, and it will be said to them: 'This glowing castle belongs to Fatima.'

She lived in such a way, putting others before herself, being that light that would outshine any darkness. Imam Ali spoke of her amazing grace openly to those who appreciated her. To one of his companions later in his life he would tell a short story of Fatima's strength, faith, and humility.

In spite of being the most beloved person to the Prophet of God, she drew water herself by means of a leather-bag, such that the mark of its strap was visible upon her chest; she swept the floor of the house to such an extent that her clothes were covered with dust; and she blew the fire below the vessel, cooking food, to such an extent that the color of her dress changed. After seeing such toil and hardship, I told her, 'You should go to the Prophet and ask for a maid who can help you in your household chores.'

So, she went to the Prophet but saw some youth with him and returned without uttering a word. The Prophet of God realized that Fatima had come to him with a request but had returned without asking him. Thus, the next morning, the Prophet himself came to our house while we were sleeping. As was his custom, saluted us three times. We thought that if we did not answer him on the third time, then he would return home as his custom was that whenever he came over, he would greet us three times requesting to enter. If he did not receive a reply, he would return.

Thus, I replied, 'And peace be upon you, O Prophet of God! Do command.' He entered therein and sat near the head of his daughter's bed and said, 'O Fatima! Yesterday you came to me, now ask what you desire dear.'

Fatima did not utter a word due to her modesty and I feared that if I would not convey her desire to him, the Prophet would get up and leave. Thus, I lifted my head and said, 'O Prophet of God! I would like to inform you that Fatima draws water by means of a leather-bag such that the mark of its strap is visible upon her chest; she mills the flour to such an extent that her hands are full of blisters; she sweeps the floor of the house to such an extent, that her clothes are covered with dust; and she blows the fire below the vessel to such an extent that the color of her dress has changed. I told her that

she should come to you and request a maid who can
help her in our household chores.'

Heavy on the Prophet's heart was the state of poverty and suffering that the Muslims were facing at his time. Not wanting to provide his family with any conveniences that the poor could not afford, he soothed his daughter with another little treasure, knowing the vastness of her faith and patience.

The Prophet replied, 'Do you want me to teach you
that which is better than a maid? When you retire for
the day, recite Allahu Akbar (God is Great) thirty-four
times, Alhamdulillah (Praise be to God) thirty-three
times, and SubhanAllah (Glory be to God) thirty-three
times.' Upon hearing this Fatima lifted her head and
said, 'I submit and am pleased with God and His
Prophet.'

Together, Ali and Fatima strived to support and comfort one another in their divine partnership, radiating light and love both to those around them, and within their home. Fatima would often find her beloved Ali working alongside her in their humble home.

On another day, the Prophet of God came to visit their humble home to find Fatima and Ali sitting next to one another. In front of them was a large pot. They were rinsing lentils together. When the Prophet saw them, he called Ali by his kunya, "Abu Al-Hasan!"

Ali replied, "At your service, O Prophet of God!"

The Prophet said to his son-in-law Ali,

Listen to me, for I say not except that which is the word of the Lord: There is not a man who helps his wife in her housework, except that with every hair on his body a whole year of worship – during which he fasted the days and kept up the nights in prayers is counted for him like the reward of the patient and the righteous.

That was the love and endurance of Ali and Fatima.

The selflessness of Lady Fatima would fill the hearts and souls of those in her midst. You could not cross the path of Fatima without being blessed. It was an impossibility to the reality of Fatima. Imagine what kind of blessing would be for those who were her students and servants? Imagine being both...

Eventually, Fiddha came into to the home of Lady Fatima to assist with some of the household chores as hired help. Some may say that she was a maid or a servant of sorts. Fatima did not see her that way. To her, she was a sister and a student. In Fiddha's eyes, Fatima was everything.

Later in her life, Fiddha would go for the Hajj pilgrimage one particular year. On her way, she got lost in the desert. Fiddha crossed paths with a man named Abdullah Mubarak. He as well seemed to have been left behind and lost his way.

"I saw a woman alone in the desert. I was riding upon a camel and went towards her... and whatever I asked her, she replied to me in the words of the Quran," Abdullah said of his encounter with Fiddha.

When Abdullah came up to Fiddha, he immediately asked her, "Who are you?"

"And say: Peace (be upon you), for they shall soon know (43:89)," she replied.

Abdullah humbly saluted her and asked, "What are you doing here?"

Fiddha answered, "And whomsoever God guides, then for him none shall beguile (39:37)."

Abdullah realized that she had lost her way.

"Are you from among the Jinn or the human beings?" Abdullah bluntly asked just to be sure who he was dealing with in this lonely desert.

"O children of Adam, put on your adornment (7:31)," Fiddha reminded.

Abdullah understood, she was definitely human.

"Where are you coming from?" Abdullah asked.

Fiddha replied with the verse, "Who are called to from a place far away (41:44)."

He could not decipher where she was coming from exactly, but realized it was not somewhere nearby.

"Where do you intend to go?" he followed.

"And for God, is incumbent upon mankind, the pilgrimage to the House (3:97)," Fiddha replied with the obligation before God.

Mecca! That is her destination, Abdullah understood.

"Since when did you part away from your caravan?"

"And indeed created We the heavens and the earth and what is between them in six days (50:38)."

Six days of separation was no easy situation. Abdullah asked if she wanted some food.

"We made them not in such bodies that do not eat, but rather require food (21:8)."

She definitely needed food, Abdullah understood.

"Well, make haste and walk quickly," Abdullah hurried her so that he could get her food.

Fiddha replied in a soft voice, "God does not impose upon any soul but to the extent of the individual's ability (2:286)."

He realized how tired she was from her reply and the weariness of her voice, which he had missed somehow, perhaps due to his attention to her replies of Quranic verse – something he had never seen before.

"Mount upon my camel, you'll ride behind my back," Abdullah innocently suggested.

"Had there been in the heavens and the earth other deities except God, they both would have been in disorder (21:22)," Fiddha bashfully replied.

Abdullah understood that she could not assent to his suggestion because of her modesty. Thus, he got off the camel and had her ride upon it in her own comfort while he walked alongside her.

When Fiddha mounted the camel she said, "Glory be to Him Who subjected this unto us (43:13)."

After riding for some time, Abdullah and Fiddha came across a traveling caravan. Abdullah turned to Fiddha and asked her to look closely at the caravan to see if she could recognize it.

"Do you think there is anyone in that caravan from among your relatives?"

"O Dawud! Verily We have appointed you a vicegerent in the Earth (38:26). And Muhammad is not but an Apostle (3:144). O Yahya! Hold thou the book fast (19:12). O Musa! Verily I am God (28:30)."

Abdullah listened closely to those names and quickly realized that there had to be men in this caravan by those names that were related to Fiddha. Abdullah ran up to the caravan and called out the names of Dawud, Muhammad, Yahya, and Musa.

Four young men came out following his voice. He brought them before Fiddha. They joyfully rushed towards her and embraced her.

"Who are these young men to you?" Abdullah asked, awaiting another majestic verse.

Fiddha smiled and said, "Wealth and children are the adornment of the life of this world (18:46)."

They were her sons.

When her sons came to her, she said to them,

"O my father! Employ him, verily the best of those whom you can employ is the strong and trusted (28:26)."

Fiddha wanted to make sure that Abdullah was compensated for his troubles with her. Her sons gave him a gift of monies as a token of their appreciation.

"And verily God gives manifold increase to whosoever He wills (2:261)," Fiddha followed.

Apparently, she wanted her sons to give him even more. Thus, they gave him more. Abdullah was baffled by her generosity, modesty, and knowledge of God's Word. As they were about to part ways Abdullah asked Fiddha's sons, "Who is she?"

"She is Fiddha, the servant of Lady Fatima the daughter of God's Prophet," one of the sons replied.

At that point in her life, it had been twenty years that Fiddha spoke nothing but the Quran. What else would be expected when she had lived alongside Fatima, the one raised by the Prophet of God, the 'City of Knowledge', the one married to Ali, the 'Gate of the City of Knowledge'.

From Fatima's sermons and traditions, to conversing with the angels, she was enlightened well beyond her years. Her vast knowledge and understanding radiated into the raising of her beloved children, empowered the minds and hearts of those living in her time, and still illuminates across centuries as it arrives to light the journey of the present.

Unrelenting patience paired with unwavering faith were also daily attributes in the days of this holy household, for both children and elders alike. The Prophet's longest living companion, Jabir ibn Abdillah Al-Ansari – who survived to see the Prophet's great grandson, spoke of a time when the Prophet had gone days without food. As it was not in the Prophet's character to ask others for things and burden them, he remained patient. There was no food in the homes of his wives or anywhere else he went. He finally went to the house of Fatima and sought to quiet his hunger. His daughter Fatima bashfully told him that she as well had no food in her home. He told her not to worry, smiled as he always had, and went on his way after some time with her.

After the Prophet left, one of Lady Fatima's neighbors brought her a gift of two loaves of bread and some meat. She thanked her neighbor for their generosity, took the food and placed it in a pot. She then covered the pot with a cloth and said, "I give preference to the Prophet of God over myself and over those with me, my husband and sons."

Lady Fatima then sent her sons Hasan and Husayn to their grandfather to tell him that food was now ready at the house. With his grandsons by his side, the Prophet returned to the house of Fatima. They all rejoiced and sat nearby. "Bring it to me," the Prophet told Fatima.

He slowly removed the cloth from atop the pot and uncovered the warm food inside. Not only was the food warm and ready to eat, but the pot was full to its brim. Fatima had only placed two loafs of bread and one small piece of meat inside the pot, but now the pot was completely full.

Jabir relates that, "We were all surprised when we saw it... I reminisce how this was one of the graces of God, and I praised and glorified God and sent blessings upon His Prophet."

The Prophet looked to his daughter with a smile so bright and wide. "Where did you get this food from?" He asked.

"From God," she replied. "Allah gives abundant sustenance to whomsoever He wills," Fatima smiled.

The Prophet sent for his son-in-law Ali to come. Ali came and others followed as well to see what the wondrous news was about.

Jabir would say, "The Messenger of God, Imam Ali, Lady Fatima, Imam Hasan, Imam Husayn, the wives of the Prophet, and other people of the house ate from the food; and still, the pot remained full of food."

Lady Fatima said, "I shall distribute this food to all of the neighbors. God has bestowed plentiful abundance to this food, just as He had offered abundance of food to Maryam."

She lived simply, but she was never poor. She walked humbly, but never destitute. She had little but gave so much. So how could anyone dare take anything from her, a divine soul with a heart so full and a spirit so warm, when she was willing to give anything she had to anyone who asked, and even more to those who did not?

CHAPTER 7

TWO SWORDS IN ONE SHEATH

Whoever holds on to you (Fatima) has held on to me, and whoever leaves you has left me. And this is because you are of me, and I am of you. You are a part of me and are my soul...

– The Prophet Muhammad

They left him even before his final moments came. At his deathbed, they mocked him and accused him of losing his mind. Lady Fatima watched as her father, the greatest man to ever walk God's green earth, was deserted by those who latched on to him during his lifetime.

"He's gone mad," some said.

"We have enough in the book of God," others muttered.

Enraged and hurt by their audacity, their Prophet ordered them away from his presence. It was not clear whether they left because of their obedience to his word, or that they had no more interest in being around a dying prophet.

Muhammad wanted only his family and loved ones around him. So, he called onto Ali, and he came forth. He took Ali's hand and then called on Fatima. She hurried towards him.

"Yes, Father?" she waited for his every call.

"Give me your hand Fatima," he said softly.

The Prophet took her hand and placed it with Ali's on his chest. He clasped his over theirs and held them tight. He did not let go. He tried to speak again but his body was just too weak. He opened his eyes to see them, but he could only keep them open for so long. Seeing him like this broke Fatima.

> *Father, O' Messenger of God, my heart is in pieces...*
> *After you who will there be for my sons? Who will*
> *there be for Ali, your brother and supporter? Who will*
> *be for God's revelation and Word?*

Fatima began to sob and fell into the embrace of the Prophet. She kissed his blessed face, which had been drenched in his own tears hearing her words. Ali and his sons joined them in their heart wrenching embrace. The Prophet held Fatima's hand and raised his head to speak to them as he gathered his strength. He placed Fatima's hand in the hand of Ali and said,

> *O' Ali, the trust of God and His Messenger is in your*
> *hand. Honor God and honor me through her. O' Ali,*
> *by God she is the Madam of the Women of Paradise,*
> *from the first to the last... O' Ali, I have not come to*
> *this point except that I asked God for her and for you,*
> *and God gave me what I asked. O' Ali, do what I told*
> *you for Fatima. For I have told her of things that Ga-*
> *briel has delivered to us. And know O' Ali, that I am*
> *pleased with whatever my daughter Fatima is pleased*
> *with, and God and His angels are also pleased.*

The Prophet then paused and said with firmness, "O' Ali, woe to whoever oppresses her. Woe to whoever infringes on her rights. Woe to whoever encroaches on her sanctity and chastity!"

Prophet Muhammad then took Fatima into his arms and held her tight. He kissed her on her head and looked into her eyes and said, "May I be sacrificed for you O' Fatima."

Fatima's eyes continued to water as Ali placed the Prophet's head upon his own chest. The Prophet's heart could not bear that he would not embrace Fatima at least once more. He held her again as his tears fell like rain soaking his grey beard.

Hasan and Husayn grasped onto the Prophet's legs and kissed him wherever they could. They cried and cried. Their father Ali wanted to remove them as to give the Prophet space and ease his pain, but the Prophet did not allow him.

"Leave them Ali. Let them be fulfilled by my presence, and let me be fulfilled by them. Let us get whatever we can of each other while we are here. For after me they will meet quakes and catastrophes. May God's curse fall upon whoever hurts them."

And what of the cries and tears of Fatima? As her tears flowed, she spoke to her father with a bleeding heart.

"My soul is a sacrifice for your soul, and may my face be a protection for yours… O' Father, will you not say another word to me as I gaze upon you? I look towards you and see you departing from us Father!"

"My daughter, I am leaving… my peace is upon you," the Prophet said as he closed his eyes.

Fatima's eyes widened. She listened to his heart, it still pounded in his chest ever so lightly. He was still breathing.

The Prophet opened his eyes again. Fatima rejoiced, tears still flowing down her soft cheeks.

"My daughter..." the Prophet spoke softly, "You are the oppressed one after me."

Fatima came in closer to the Prophet as he gave her his last words.

> Whoever hurts you has hurt me, and whoever pleases you has pleased me. Whoever holds on to you has held on to me, and whoever leaves you has left me. And this is because you are of me, and I am of you. You are a part of me and are my soul...

The Prophet said this with tears in his eyes as he gazed at his daughter's face for the last time. Then he promised her with his solemn words.

"To my Lord I go and complain of your oppressors that are from my nation..."

Holding the Prophet in his arms, Ali felt his body loosen and then Ali knew. In those moments, Ali would rise and say, "May God give you patience, for He has taken His Prophet back to Him."

The room erupted in wails and cries that shook the mountains of Mecca and the plains of Medina. But no cries and no wails were like that of Fatima. No heart endured what her heart did of pain and agony over the death of her father Muhammad. Fatima mourned her father with the following lines.

O' Father, your Lord took you back to Him

O' Father, your home is now Heaven

O' Father, to Gabriel we mourn and cry

O' Father, your Lord called, and you would reply

Imam Ali and Lady Fatima took to the burial rituals and held the funeral. The funeral was too small for a man of his stature. "Where are his people? Where are his companions?" one would ask. Fatima was too consumed with honoring her father and grieving over his loss to concern herself with others. But the fact of the matter remained, where were they?

A short distance away and beneath a tent, the schemes and mischief had begun, possibly, because the truth shone too evident under the open sky. It was under that tent of Banu Saidah that the Ansar found themselves gathered. The meeting place in short became known as Saqeefa. There they deliberated over who was going to take charge as the new head of state for the growing Muslim nation. Saad bin Ubadah was the Ansar's man. They wanted him to succeed the Prophet. Though he was ill, they still brought him lying on a bed to Saqeefa to make his claim.

He delivered a speech from his bed and invited the Ansar to pledge allegiance to him. All the Ansar accepted his call and said to one another as follows:

If the Muhajiroun say that they have migrated along with the Prophet from Mecca to Medina, while they

are the foremost companions of the Prophet and are
from his family, and question why we dispute with
them regarding the caliphate and sovereignty after the
death of the Prophet, then what shall we reply to them?

Some of them would respond amongst themselves saying, "We will reply to their objection by saying, 'Let there be one commander from among us and one from among you.' We will not accept any proposal other than this."

Almost disgusted at their proposal, Saad said in a meek voice, "This is the first weakness manifest in you."

Umar ibn Al-Khattab heard of what was transpiring at Saqeefa. He quickly called for Abu Bakr to come forth. Abu Bakr told him he was not available, but Umar insisted.

"An incident has occurred for which your presence is a must, therefore hasten immediately," Umar's message read.

Abu Bakr made haste and met with Umar.

"What is going on?" Abu Bakr asked Umar as soon as he saw him.

Umar pulled him closer.

Don't you know that the Ansar have gathered at the
Saqeefa of Bani Saidah and are determined to hand
over rulership to Saad bin Ubadah, while a good man
from among them suggested that, let there be one
commander from among us and one from among
you?!

Without much further exchange they rushed towards Saqeefa. When they arrived, they found a huge gathering of men. Umar wanted to quickly speak and address the situation. Abu Bakr grabbed him and whispered, "Slow down, let me address them first, thereafter you may say what you wish."

Umar assented and was, in the end, pleased with Abu Bakr's words. Abu Bakr spoke,

> *Allah, the Almighty, chose Muhammad as a prophet, a messenger and a guide for the people and He made him a witness over the Ummah until they worshipped the One God and abandoned polytheism, while previously people had chosen various deities for themselves and worshipped them. They believed that these deities would intercede for them and give them benefit. However, these statues were made of carved stones and wood, and they worshiped other gods besides Allah which can neither hurt them nor profit them.*

> *But it was hard for the Arabs to forsake the religion of their forefathers. Allah the Merciful, then granted this distinction upon the Muhajiroun to be the first ones to hasten to his call and believe in him. They generously rose up to defend him, and in this way they endured and bore patiently the severities, tortures, and belying of the polytheists. The Muhajiroun were the foremost to worship Allah upon this earth and they were the first ones to believe in Allah and His Prophet.*

The Muhajiroun are the friends and relatives of the Prophet and are more liable to hold authority over the masses after his death, while the one who opposes them regarding this matter is an oppressor! O group of Ansar, you are not among those who deny their distinction and superiority in religion and their precedence in (accepting) Islam. Allah chose you to be the companions and friends of the religion and the Messenger, and commanded the Prophet to migrate towards you. Most of his wives and companions were from among you, while none equals you in our eyes after the foremost Muhajiroun and thus we are the commanders, and you are the ministers. We will not refrain from taking your advice and we will not issue orders without consulting you in the affairs.

Umar stared the men down as he saw looks of contentment and faces of irritation. One of the Ansar stood up and spoke loudly to the men present.

O group of Ansar! Hold fast to your affairs for there are men under your command ready to strike anyone, while no one has the audacity to oppose you regarding it, and none has the power to take the reins of affairs in their hands without your order and consent. You are the ones possessed with honor, splendor, manpower, potential and personality. People turn to you for their tasks and for advice, so do not dispute among yourselves otherwise, the result of your affairs will be ruined! If the Muhajiroun do not accept what I said

and what you heard, then our opinion is that one man
from among us may be chosen as a guide and one man
from among them.

Umar quickly ascended to respond to these sentiments.

Far be it! There cannot be two swords in one sheath
and the Arabs will never consent to this. The Ansar
may be their guides for the reason that the Prophet's
clan was different from that of yours, while the 'Arabs
do not differ in the matter that the guide should be
from the same clan as that of the Prophet. Then who is
it that disputes with us regarding the affairs of the authority that is the right of the Prophet, while we are the
friends and relatives of the Prophet."

The room only grew more tense. Each member of the gathering looking to the other unsure what will happen next. Hubab
would come back with a rebuttal.

O group of Ansar! Take care of your opinion and do
not accept the words of this man and his companions
as they desire to snatch away the authority from your
destiny! If they oppose you, then remove them from
your city for you are most worthy of authority! If expelling them from Medina requires the use of the
sword, then do so. Men are in approval and steadfast
with you, while I stand in this way as a solid pillar and
an unagreeable flaw against them. To straighten the affairs, I insist to be similar to the stick that is erected in
the sleeping-place of the camels upon which they rub

the dirt off their bodies. I am similar to a palm-tree that rests upon a wall or a pillar, and I am like a lion that does not fear anyone. I possess the heart of a lion. By Allah! If you wish I will turn around his limb.

Umar would rise up and shout out, "Then may Allah kill you!"

Hubab replied with the same spite, "May He kill you!"

The men were at each other's throats. They were being pulled back by their comrades. In all the commotion, Abu Ubaydah shouts at them, "You were one of those who were the foremost to help the Prophet in your city! Do not be the first ones to make changes and alterations in Islam!"

Bashir bin Saad would rise up and say to his brethren, "O group of Ansar! Beware that Muhammad is related to the Quraysh, he was their kinsman and their near one. By Allah! You shall not find me differing with them in regard to the matters of authority."

The matter was getting closer to the Muhajiroun.

"Here are Umar and Abu Ubaydah, you may pledge allegiance at the hand of the one whom you desire," boldly stated Abu Bakr turning the tables to an ultimatum to be decided swiftly.

Abu Bakr's companions refused his offer.

By Allah! We will not precede you in taking the affairs of the caliphate in our hands. You are the best of the Muhajiroun, while you were the vicegerent of the

*Prophet in offering the prayers, which is the best com-
mand of religion. Now extend your hand so that we
may pledge allegiance at your hands.*

Extend his hand he did, and that hand was kissed first by
Bashir ibn Saad, even before Umar and Abu Ubaydah. Hubab al-
Ansari changed colors and yelled out at Ibn Saad.

"O Bashir! May dust be upon your head! You have acted
stingy in the matter that your cousin (Saad bin Ubadah) may become the commander!"

By order of the Aws clan's chief, all their tribesmen then gave
allegiance to Abu Bakr. The Khazraj tribe did the same. In moments, Saad bin Ubadah was destroyed. He lay in his bed disoriented as to how quickly things changed. He was almost crushed
by the swarm of men that disregarded him, and almost trampled
on his body killing him as they rushed to pay allegiance to the
new leader.

"Hey! You're going to kill me!" He called out to the heedless
men.

Umar scoffed and said, "Kill Saad, may Allah kill him!"

Qays bin Saad, who was at his father's side, jumped up and
grabbed Umar by his grey beard. '

"By Allah, O son of Sahhak! You are the one who runs away
from battle in fear, but among ordinary people and at times of
peace you behave like a lion! If you move even a single hair of
the head of my father, then you shall not return but that I will fill

your face with wounds such that the bones thereof will be visible!"

Abu Bakr instructed Umar to stop and not to react. "Remain calm and act cautiously, for caution is better and more profitable," Abu Bakr ordered Umar.

Qays released Umar. His father looked up towards him with pure anger and spite.

> *O son of Sahhak! By Allah! If I had the strength to stand up and if I had not been sick, indeed you and Abu Bakr would have heard my roaring, like a lion, in the streets of Medina, and you would have fled from Medina in fear! I would have joined ranks with a group of men through whom you would be degraded and subjugated not like the present circumstances in which others will be under your command. O children of Khazraj! Take me away from this place of commotion.*

They lifted Saad up from his bed and took him to his house.

***

It was only a few moons ago and across the golden sands of Arabia that atop a man-made hill of stones and saddles, stood the Prophet of God, raising the hand of Ali in his. Before them was a gathering of thousands of warm hearts in a land called Ghadir Khum. Men and women stood cheering the name of Ali, pledging allegiance to him and acceptance of a divine order of the Lord. "Whoever I am his master, Ali is his master," the Prophet proclaimed.

In Ali's leadership, as the heir-apparent of the Prophet of God, it was decreed that the voice of the oppressed would be heard, support to the poor would be safeguarded, and justice for the marginalized would be realized.

In his guardianship was to be the warmth for the orphans, the freedom of the slaves, and the resonance of the Word of God. Even though the event of Ghadir Khum was witnessed and documented across all groups and tribes, the attempts to muffle the divine decree, silence the oppressed, and hush the crowds had begun.

The betrayal of the Prophet of God would continue. The suppression of the universe within Ali would persist. The oppression of the light within Fatima would deepen.

And Saqeefa is where the people were. Not at the Prophet's bedside or mourning with his family. They were not paying condolences to his daughter Fatima and son-in-law Ali. They were not tending to the burial rituals and reciting Quran over his body. They were at Saqeefa deciding who would fill the Prophet's shoes, even before the shoes were removed from his feet. That was Saqeefa. For every woe and every grief, would come from Saqeefa.

CHAPTER 8

BURN THE HOUSE

I swear by Allah, that if the command of Allah would not have been decreed and the promise to bear patiently had not been given to me by the Prophet, I would have crushed your skulls.

– Imam Ali

While the event of allegiance to the new caliph transpired, Imam Ali was busy preparing the grave of the Prophet. A man came up to him with the news, and Ali was seen carrying a shovel in his hand. As he plowed the earth that would swallow Muhammad's body, unsettled by the thought, the man wished to deliver to Ali the update on the people's decision.

> *People have sworn allegiance to Abu Bakr, while the Ansar have been defeated in the matter of choosing the caliph, for a dispute arose among themselves. Al-Tulaqaa' (those who had been freed by the Prophet during the conquest of Mecca) took precedence and swore allegiance to Abu Bakr, they did not seek your advice because you were absent.*

Imam Ali put the shovel down in the ground, still holding on to its handle in his palm. He remembered God, as he always had.

In the name of Allah, the Beneficent, the Merciful. Alif Lam Mim. What! Do people imagine that they will be left off on (their) saying: 'We believe', and they will not be tried? And indeed We did try those before them, and Allah certainly knows those who are truthful, and certainly He knows the liars. Or imagine they who work evil that they will escape Us? Ill is what they judge! (29:1-4)

Soon after this announcement, Abu Sufyan of the Umayyads made his way to the house of the Prophet. Imam Ali and his uncle Abbas bin Abdulmuttalib were present inside. He entered the home reciting verses of poetry with a braying voice in a façade of anguish for the family of Muhammad.

O' Banu Hashim! Do not let others have greed for the caliphate, particularly the people of the clans of Taym bin Murrah (Abu Bakr) and Adi (Umar) for the affair is only your right and will return to you. O Abal Hasan (Ali)! Clench your claws and prepare yourself, for you are more worthy for the affair and that of what you desire!

O' Banu Hashim! O children of 'Abdul Manaf! Do you agree that Abu Bakr, the lowly and son of the lowly, may rule over you? By Allah! If you desire, I can gather such a large army of horsemen and foot soldiers that they will put him and supporters in a fix!

Imam Ali was not moved by his words. He knew Abu Sufyan's intentions. He faced him in battle before and upon the

Conquest of Mecca, knew that Abu Sufyan had no other choice but to come into the fold of Islam. The Umayyad Chief was nothing more than a half-time wheeling-dealing crook that was bent on causing mischief and mayhem for the followers of Muhammad.

"Go back, I swear by Allah that whatever you say is not for the sake of Allah! You are always in a state of deceit and playing tricks against Islam and the Muslims," Ali responded firmly. "We are attending the funeral of the Prophet, and everyone will reach the reward of their good deeds, and Allah is the Guardian and Helper of the oppressed." There was no toying with Ali.

Abu Sufyan was taken aback and disappointed that he could not even gain a few inches of traction with his plan. He left Imam Ali and went towards the Mosque of the Prophet, where he mixed and mingled with others from various tribes. More and more he spoke of power and less and less about the Prophet. Satan was ever so present at the Prophet's death. He slithered and slid in between the people, whispering to them affairs of desire and power.

"Now is your chance," he suggested. "It is your right," he said. God's Word was neglected, His people afflicted with pain and sorrow, and His cause orphaned.

For days, Ali did not come out of his house. The people had gathered around Abu Bakr and paid him allegiance, while Ali's close companions and the sons of Banu Hashem refused and stayed home.

Ali would turn to the Ansar to see if they would be of any assistance in this ordeal.

In the night, Ali and Fatima would go together to potential supporters in their community, advocating for the wellbeing of the people. Fatima sat upon a mount, escorted by her valiant husband Ali, and took to the Ansar. She would remind them of the divine plan for good, one ordained by the All-Merciful Lord for the betterment of humanity – not one chosen by tribes and drenched in human motives and schemes. And was Fatima's word not the word of the Prophet? In her status as the Prophet's daughter and beloved, Fatima exemplified what it meant to be courage itself, taking a stand as a woman and a member of society, standing up and protecting the right of Ali, which in turn was the right of the people to be lead justly, compassionately, and honorably. She spoke to them passionately and evoked the greatest empathy and emotion. However, their reply was far from what they wished for.

"O daughter of the Prophet of Allah! We have taken the oath of allegiance to Abu Bakr and the die has been cast. If your cousin and husband had approached us in the beginning, before we had given the allegiance to Abu Bakr, we would have supported him and listened to him regarding the caliphate," they replied meekly.

"In that case, should I have left the corpse of the Prophet in his house unburied and come to you to dispute with men regarding the caliphate?" Ali scolded the men for such a foolish suggestion. As if, when just twenty-three years earlier, they had forgotten that they lived in a state of endless warfare, lack of order and justice, and even burying their daughters alive. As if, they had forgotten that from the Prophet's lap to the day of Ghadir on the golden sands, Ali was groomed to be the leader and warrior of the nation, illuminating light to every corner that was devoured by darkness. As if, they could believe that a prophet as wise, self-less, and merciful as their Prophet Muhammad could leave them alone and leaderless.

From atop of her mount Fatima then assured the people before her.

"Abu Al-Hasan was bound and more befitting to accomplish the funeral proceedings of the Prophet, while the Muhajiroun and Ansar have committed such an act that Allah will reprimand and punish them for," Fatima promised.

Sitting upon the makeshift throne quickly assembled for the new Caliph in the Prophet's Mosque, Abu Bakr contemplated the steps ahead. Ali's allegiance was key. He knew that, and Umar made sure that he remembered.

"Why do you not send a message to Ali to come and pay allegiance at your hands? Everyone has sworn allegiance except him and four others."

Abu Bakr was more careful and moderate in his approach to things than Umar. He spoke softly and possessed a calm demeanor. Umar did not see the utility in that. His method was to get things done as he saw them, and to do so by any means necessary. His tongue was sharp, piercing the hardest of stone, and his touch was far from gentle.

"I am sending Qunfudh to bring Ali," Umar told Abu Bakr. Qunfudh was one of Abu Bakr's freed slaves and became one of Umar's fiercest men. Like him, his approach to things was heavy-handed and far from diplomatic.

Qunfudh led a group of men tasked by Umar to go to the House of Ali and demand he pay allegiance to the new Caliphate. Off they went to the humble home of Fatima and Ali, banged on the door, and called out to its owners.

"Come out O' Ali! You are hereby summoned by the Caliph to pay allegiance! Come out!" Qunfudh yelled.

Imam Ali refused.

"Allow us permission to come inside and speak with you then, for the Caliph of the Prophet of God has called you," the men replied.

Ali replied, "How soon do you attribute a lie to the Prophet?" Ali again refused and turned them away with the following message to Abu Bakr.

"It is not possible for me to step outside. For I am busy compiling the Quran that you have abandoned, while you have attached yourselves to this world. I have sworn that I will not step out of the house, nor wear my cloak until I finish compiling the Quran."

Qunfudh and his men returned with the message to the new Caliph. They explained that Ali would not allow them to enter his house, nor would he step outside to go with them and pay allegiance.

"He also asked, 'How soon do you attribute a lie to the Prophet?' when we called you the Caliph of God's Prophet," Qunfudh added.

Abu Bakr was shaken by those words and began to weep. Umar grew in anger and nudged the leader he helped elect.

"Do not give relief to this debaucher!" Umar snapped.

Abu Bakr wiped away his tears and ordered the men, "Go to Ali and tell him that the Commander of the Faithful has invited you to come to him and take the oath of allegiance."

They came to the door of the house once again and called out to Ali.

"O' Ali, the Commander of the Faithful has invited you to come to him and take the oath of allegiance as the people have done. Come with us," the men said.

"Commander of the Faithful?" Ali thought to himself. That was a title that the Holy Prophet had given to Ali, and him alone. It was a title of honor he earned and no one else shared with him. Fatima also heard the men as they used those words for a man who did not own the title. She wanted to get up and respond herself, but Ali addressed the matter himself swiftly.

Ali raised his voice in worship like the mountain lion he was. "Glory be to God! He claims that which is not his!"

Returning to Abu Bakr, Qunfudh relayed Ali's response. Hearing Ali's words again brought Abu Bakr to tears. Umar was becoming impatient with both Abu Bakr's tears and Ali's scolding.

"Go back to the house of Ali and bring him here now! If he refuses, then enter without permission," Umar ordered Qunfudh.

Qunfudh returned to the house of Ali.

At arrival he yelled out, "Ali! You must come with us, open the door at once!"

Inside, Ali was sitting with his sons and companions. About to reply to the men and send them away once again, Lady Fatima came to her husband and told him not to bother. Fatima had enough of these men who disrespected her home. She would answer the door and tell the men to go away, perhaps they would respect her wishes as the daughter of their prophet.

"I forbid you to enter my home," she said and made her presence known. The men were taken aback by the voice of Fatima. The Prophet's daughter then stood near the door facing the group that had gathered in front of her house. Fatima delivered a fiery speech for all those present to hear.

> I have not known a group more ill-mannered than you! You left the corpse of the Prophet in our midst and took the affairs of appointing a leader into your own hands! You did not seek our advice and rather, neglected our rights. Perhaps you pretended to not know the event of Ghadir. By Allah! On that day, the Prophet of Allah took the pledge from the people regarding the friendship and authority of Ali. The Messenger did that so you would never desire to take the

authority in your own hands, but you scraped the re-
lation with your Prophet by doing so. Surely Allah is
the Judge between us and you in this world and in the
hereafter!

Even hearts of stone took a moment of pause with her words. They knew the truth, that divine matters that pertained to leading and guiding human lives were not things to meddle with. Fatima returned to the interior of her home, while the men remained outside looking at one another dumbfounded. Qunfudh sent some of his men back to Abu Bakr to inform him that it was Fatima this time who turned them away.

Hearing the news, Umar was outraged.

"What do we have to do with the tasks of women!" He bellowed. While Abu Bakr wept of his calamity, Umar got up from his place in a fiery craze.

"Gather the firewood!" he called to his men and marched on to the House of Fatima. They picked up the wood from wherever they could and followed Umar. Upon his arrival he told his men to stack the wood upon the walls of the house.

"Ali! Come out O' Ali!" Umar yelled out from outside.

Silence. There was no response.

"What do you intend on doing sir?" Qunfudh asked Umar intently.

"By Allah! If you do not step out O' Ali, and swear allegiance at the hands of the caliph of the Prophet of Allah, I shall burn you down."

Lady Fatima was behind the door at this point. She answered him with a question, perhaps an appeal to the humanity in his heart.

"Why do you deal with us in this manner, Umar?"

Umar rolled his eyes and only grew louder in his fury.

"I said, open the door or else I will burn this house down!"

One of the men turned to the man in charge, and hesitantly stated, "But Fatima is inside sir."

"So what?!" he yelled back.

"Do you not fear Allah still and persist in wanting to enter my house?" Lady Fatima replied calmly but firmly.

He had enough.

"Bring me fire!" he ordered his men.

They grabbed their torches and with their hands set fire to the house of Fatima. Smoke began to seep inside, and Fatima would cough as she stood close behind the door. The flames grew upon the old wooden entrance, and its clasp weakened. The men stepped back and thrusted forward with their shoulders to push the door open. They did so with such force that the door flung open, and with Fatima behind it, she was crushed between the door and the wall.

Fatima fell to the ground and called out, "O' Father, O' Prophet of Allah!"

The men entered the house with a craze in their eyes. Allegiance to the caliphate had to be obtained, no matter the cost.

They saw Fatima on the ground. One of the men removed his horse whip from his belt and struck Fatima with it. From the pain and heat of the lash, Fatima let out a heart wrenching cry. Everything happened so abruptly, a darkness erupting within, suffocating the light and love within Fatima's home. The man then unsheathed his sword.

"Fatima?!" Ali called out.

Imam Ali rushed in from the back of the house. He found the man standing above his beloved with whip and sword in hand, while smokey flames filled the background. Ali charged at him like a lion upon its prey. He grabbed the man by the throat with his iron grasp and threw him to the other side of the room. Slammed into the ground, his neck twisted, and the side of his face was cut open.

"Send more men here at once!" they cried out to the soldiers outside.

Within moments, dozens of men encircling the house obliged. As they surrounded Ali, they saw the Prophet's daughter on the ground, and their eyes widened like the horizon. Some held back their tears, but they could not hold back the grief in their hearts and their utter shock to see Fatima in such a state.

The children rushed to shield their injured mother, their little arms and falling tears covering her. Fatima laid on the ground with arms wrapped around her abdomen, worried that something had happened to her unborn child. She was six months pregnant. They had already given their baby a name. They would call him Muhsin, a name fit for a prince, symbolizing benevolence and beauty.

Fatima's children Hasan, Husayn, Zaynab and Umm Kulthoom sobbed at the sight of their mother's agony. At her side, trying to protect her, they were terrified before these men in swords. Men whose hearts spewed fear and enmity that ripped away the warmth and safety that the children basked in.

Imam Ali lifted his wife's aggressor by the collar with one hand, while he unsheathed his sword with the other. Gasping for air, he could not utter a word. Before killing him, Ali stopped himself. Though he had the strength of forty-men, he did not have his 'forty-men'.

In those moments, time slowed, bringing forth a memory. Before the Prophet passed, he told Ali, "You will face troubles after me… Lest you have forty-men to support you, do not rise, and choose patience…"

Ali let go of the man's throat and dropped his sword. As the man gasped for air, Ali looked down at him and made it crystal clear.

"I swear by Allah, that if the command of Allah would not have been decreed and the promise to bear patiently had not been given to me by the Prophet, I would have crushed your skulls."

As he struggled to get back to his feet, the chief among them finally stood up and faced Ali.

"Take him away!" he ordered.

The men chained the Lion of God and dragged him out of the house. Ali did not resist. The children's cries and screams filled the air of smoke and fire.

"Baba!" they called out, as the men walked on past the injured body of their mother Fatima.

Ali was dragged across Medina like an injured lion in chains. People gasped at the sight of Ali ibn Abi Talib taken as a prisoner of the caliphate. Brought before Abu Bakr at the Mosque of the Prophet like a slave of conquest, Ali was presented before the new Caliph to be judged. His movement was confined having been chained at the wrists and ankles. Standing behind the new Caliph was a row of his armed commanders.

From right to left they could be seen: Khalid bin Al-Walid, Abu Ubaydah Al-Jarrah, Salim the freed slave of Abu Hudhay-fah, Ma'adh bin Jabal, Al-Mughirah bin Shu'bah, Usayd bin Hudhayr, and Bashir bin Saad. Umar stood at the head of Imam Ali with his sword unsheathed, like a hunter parading his game. Yet, he knew very well that he was no hunter in this game.

"Swear the oath of allegiance to Abu Bakr!" they ordered Ali.

"I will not do so," Ali replied as he looked away.

They said, "By Allah! If you do not swear the oath of allegiance, we will strike your head."

Lifting his head and looking at Abu Bakr, Ali replied, "In this way you will have killed the servant of Allah and the brother of the Prophet of Allah."

"Servant of Allah, perhaps, but the brother of the Prophet of Allah, I say not!" Umar replied.

"Just pay allegiance Ali," another one of the men said.

Ali did not look at Umar or the other men. He looked straight at Abu Bakr, who was seated in front of him. Ali straightened his posture with his head held high and spoke to the delegation as he would speak from the pulpit.

> I am more worthy of the caliphate than you, I shall not swear allegiance at your hands when it is more fitting that you swear allegiance to me. But you have taken the position by your own hands! You snatched the caliphate away from the Ansar on the grounds that you are the Prophet's relatives, and thus in reality you usurped the rights from us – the Family of the Prophet!
>
> Did you not put forward this claim in front of the Ansar, that you were more entitled to succeed Muhammad being his 'close relatives'? Thus, the Ansar handed over the authority to you and surrendered. Now I put forward the same claim that you put forth to the Ansar. I was nearer to the Prophet in his lifetime and even now after his death. Then deal justly with us if you possess faith, or else you intentionally seek refuge in oppression.

Abu Bakr's silence only grew louder.

Umar jumped back in and emphasized, "We shall not release you until you swear allegiance to Abu Bakr!"

Imam Ali turned to Umar and scoffed.

"Milk thou and keep half for yourself, and strive for him today, for tomorrow he shall return it to you."

The tension in the room was unbearable.

Back at their home, stood Fatima and her children. She gathered herself, suppressing her pain, and took the hands of her children in hers. She made her way towards the Mosque of the Prophet where her husband Ali was being held captive.

She entered the Mosque and took in the scene. The Lion of God chained at the wrists and ankles, placed before the Caliph for questioning. Around him stood the Caliph's men looking down on him like an enemy of the newly founded state.

"Do you intend to take my husband away from me, making me a widow?" Fatima called out to Abu Bakr as she entered the Mosque.

She walked in closer. "If you do not release him, I swear by Allah, I will dishevel my hair and tear my collar. I will go to the grave of my father and pray to Allah against you."

The men stood there without an utterance. Without waiting long for a response, Fatima walked out and proceeded towards the grave of the Prophet. If they did not know what the prayers of Fatima could do to the people of Medina, Ali surely did.

"Salman!" Ali called his companion to come forth at once. Awaiting his orders nearby, Salman came quickly.

Go forth and stop Fatima! It is as if I see the two sides of Medina trembling and swallowed by the earth. By

God, if Fatima dishevels her hair and tears the collar of
her shirt while at the grave of the Prophet to imprecate
to Allah, the people of Medina will not get any respite
and they will all be swallowed up by the ground!

The rest of the men continued to stand in shock, as if para-
lyzed by the reality that could soon be theirs. Salman rushed to
catch up with Fatima who had swiftly made her way to the
Prophet's grave. Her prayers had already begun. The walls of
Medina began to tremble and the earth beneath them would
shake.

Salman finally got to her. Almost out of breath he managed
to say, "O daughter of Muhammad! Allah has made your father
a mercy for the worlds! Please return to your home and do not
imprecate."

Fatima turned to Salman.

"O Salman! They desire to kill Ali and my patience has now
parted, let me be at the grave of my father… so I can pray to
Allah," she replied.

"I fear that Medina will tremble due to your prayers and the
earth will swallow up everyone. Ali himself has sent me to return
you back. He requested that you refrain from imprecating my
Lady," Salman pleaded.

Fatima lowered her praying hands and nodded her head. The
words of Ali were not the words of any ordinary man. They had
the foresight and depth of one who holds the weight of humanity's wellbeing upon his shoulders.

"I will return, forebear, listen and obey Ali."

While Salman worked to hold back Lady Fatima from imprecating, the Caliph's men looked at each other in despair. After hearing Fatima's declaration, one of the men turned to the Caliph with a concerned look.

"What do you intend to do? Do you wish to bring perdition upon everyone?"

Abu Bakr could not take that risk. He knew the power of Fatima. He could not gamble with it more than he already had. Thus, he ordered Ali's release. The Caliph's men unchained Ali and let him be. Ali walked to the Prophet's grave where he found Fatima and their sons and daughters weeping. He too joined them in their cries.

They sobbed at the Prophet's grave and prayed for their nation. As if the departure of the Prophet was not enough of a hardship to shatter the hearts of his family. Their wounds were scathed deeper and their sorrow heavier within.

"My brother... the people did reckon me weak and had tried to kill me," Ali said in a sorrowful voice as he looked down at the Holy Prophet's grave.

Ali took the hands of his wife and children and made his way back to their home. A home that was found in shambles from the torches and fire. A home that was violated and desecrated.

***

Many days after this entire ordeal, Umar and Abu Bakr sat with one another reflecting on the events that had passed. Much had transpired and greater unease took over the hearts of the Caliph and his men.

"Let us go to Fatima as we have angered her," Umar said to Abu Bakr. "The matter of the land of Fadak has not helped either."

"Yes, we should go now," Abu Bakr replied as he stood up.

They went to her house and asked permission to enter. Lady Fatima refused them permission. Rejected, they went about to find Ali and ask him to intercede on their behalf.

"Please, give us an audience with Fatima," they pleaded.

After asking Fatima, Ali allowed them to come forth to their home. They entered and gave salutations to Fatima. She did not reply. Instead, she turned her back and would not look at them. Though Medina was known for its heat, they felt cold like they never had before.

Abu Bakr came a bit closer and beseeched Lady Fatima.

"O beloved of the Prophet of God! By God, the family of the Prophet is dearer to me than my own family, and I hold you dearer to myself than my daughter Aisha, and I had wished that on the day the Prophet died I would have died in his place and would not have survived him.

"Do you perceive that despite being aware of your excellence, I would keep you away from your rights and inheritance at this moment? It is only that I have heard your father say, 'We prophets do not leave anything as inheritance, and whatever is left behind is charity.'"

Still not looking at them, Fatima did not reply. They waited a bit more.

"Then if I narrate to you from my father, will you act according to it?" finally she replied.

"Yes, of course," they replied.

"I put you on an oath before Allah, haven't you heard the Prophet say, 'The pleasure of Fatima is my pleasure, and her discontent is my discontent. Then the one who loves Fatima, my daughter, loves me. The one who pleases Fatima, pleases me, and the one who angers Fatima angers me.'"

"Yes, indeed we have heard this from the Prophet," they said.

"I hold Allah and the angels witness, that you have angered me and displeased me and when I meet the Prophet of Allah, I will complain to him regarding the both of you!"

The Caliph could not control his response. He felt as if the earth was swallowing him where he stood.

"I seek refuge of Allah from His anger and that of yours O Fatima!" he cried out. His tears flowing down his cheeks and visibly shaking from his shoulders to his knees.

Fatima knew that between the words and tears, their schemes and betrayals would continue to devastate the lives of all those who stood for truth, from her own life to her children, to the nation, and to all those to come.

"I swear by Allah, I will make prayers against you after every prayer," Fatima promised, unmoved by the tears that he shed.

Their pleas were not accepted nor were they appreciated. Fatima could not look at them and instead asked them to leave. Abu Bakr exited the home of Ali and Fatima in a hysterical daze, weeping as if he had witnessed the massacre of his family and kinsmen. People gathered around to see what was going on. Encircling him, they waited for him to address them.

"Each one of you men lie in bed with your wives at night and embrace each other and live happily with your relatives and leave me alone in this conflict. I do not need your allegiance – break the oath of allegiance that you have sworn at my hands!"

A few loyalists would quickly reply to the Caliph's unexpected request.

"O vicegerent of the Prophet! The caliphate is incomplete without you! You are more informed than us in the affairs. If you remove yourself from the caliphate, the religion will be destroyed!"

Abu Bakr wiped his tears and looked upon them.

"By Allah! Had I not feared that the rope of religion would be weakened, I would not have slept in a state with the oath of allegiance of even one Muslim upon myself, after having heard the words of Fatima."

They left the house of Fatima. The caliphate was not recused nor was authority returned to the House of the Prophet. Fatima did not care for those tears, as their actions spoke much louder than the cries of elderly men.

The Caliph and his men apparently did not stop at trying to force Ali's hand to pledge allegiance. They took the inheritance of Lady Fatima and claimed it as property of the state. Fatima's anger was not for land though, it was for an utter disregard to the sanctity of the Prophet and the religion he sacrificed everything to bring forth and preserve. Was there not anyone to rise against this ordeal? Were there not men of God to come forth and answer the call of truth?

CHAPTER 9

THE TWELVE MEN

If I had with me men who were true supporters of Allah, the Mighty, the Sublime, and His Prophet, equaling the number of these sheep, I would certainly have deposed this one from his authority...

– Imam Ali

The caliphate was not established unopposed. The Prophet prescribed to Ali in his will that he should expect to be opposed and that people would take what is rightfully his to hold and spread justice with. He told Ali not to rise against such opposition unless he had forty firm supporters behind him, otherwise he would risk breaking apart the religion that was still in its early stages of infancy. Islam was not strong enough to withhold such a schism unless that support was found in such a manner. Though Ali and Fatima did not have forty men behind them to rise up against those who usurped their rights, there were valiant men who could not sit idly by. They were the Twelve Men.

They were equally split between men from the Muhajiroun and men from the Ansar. The six from amongst the Muhajiroun were Khalid ibn Said ibn al-Aas, Salman al-Farsi, Abuthar al-Ghafari, Miqdad ibn al-Aswad, 'Ammar ibn Yasir and Buraydah al-Aslami. The other six men from amongst the Ansar were Abul Haytham ibn al-Tihan, Sahl ibn Hunayf, Uthman ibn Hunayf,

Khuzaymah ibn Thabit Dhus Shahadatain, Ubayy ibn Kaab and Abu Ayyub al-Ansari.

As soon as Abu Bakr ascended the pulpit in the Mosque of the Prophet, the Twelve Men gathered and shared their opinions on the matter. Some of them said, "By Allah, we shall go to Abu Bakr and bring him down from the pulpit of the Prophet!"

Others were a bit more prudent in their approach and thought otherwise.

Some said, "If we do this, we shall doom our own selves. Allah says in the Qur'an, 'And cast not yourselves with your own hands into perdition.' (2:195) It is better that we go to the Commander of the Faithful Ali and seek his advice regarding this matter."

They consented to that sentiment. Thus, the Twelve Men went to Imam Ali who was still diligently working on the compilation of the Quran and its verses. One of the men came forward after giving dutiful salutations to their leader and said,

> O Commander of the Faithful! Indeed, you are the best and worthiest for the caliphate among the people – for we have heard the Prophet say that Ali is with the truth and the truth is with Ali, and the truth turns wherever Ali turns. We have decided to go to Abu Bakr and bring him down from the pulpit of the Prophet and have come to seek your advice in this regard… We will do whatever you say.

Imam Ali gazed upon these valiant men.

If you do what you are intending to do, then fights will erupt with you, and you are less in number. The community has gathered and forsaken the words of their Prophet and have attributed falsehood to Allah. I have counselled with my family regarding this, and they have decided to remain silent for they are aware of the resentment and enmity of the opponents towards Allah and the Household of the Prophet. The enemies pursue the hostility of the Days of Ignorance and desire to seek vengeance from those days.

The men nodded their heads, each carrying a solemn look on his face, aware of the weight of the task ahead. Ali continued,

Go to Abu Bakr and relay to him whatever you have heard about me from the Prophet. Through this, clear the doubt from his mind as this will prove to be greater evidence for him. Ultimately his punishment will increase on the Day when he is brought in front of Allah, for he has disobeyed His Messenger and opposed Him.

The Twelve Men marched on to the Mosque. It was a Friday and the fourth day after the Prophet's passing. Each one of them possessed the fearlessness of a warrior and the stature of a scholar. They stood before the pulpit and watched the Caliph walk towards it. As he got closer to the pulpit, the men took turns in singing the praises of Ali ibn Abi Talib. Each of them quoted the Prophet in his praises and tributes to Ali.

The first one to come forward was Khalid ibn Said ibn al-Aas and he was followed by the other emigrants, and then the Ansar came forward. By the time the Caliph sat on the pulpit, he was dizzy with the praises of Ali ibn Abi Talib. He could not muster up an intelligent response to the men's assertions, nor could he refute them.

"You are more worthy of authority and I am not the best one among you, leave me, leave me!" he yelled out.

The sight of Abu Bakr being so disoriented and lacking any sort of wit exasperated his comrades. Umar could not tolerate such a feeble position for the new caliphate. When he heard the Caliph's reply to Ali's men he shouted:

> Come down from the pulpit, you ignoble! If you do not
> have the power to reply to the arguments of Quraysh,
> why have you taken the seat of the caliphate?! By Allah!
> I resolve to depose you from this position and hand it
> over to Salim, the freed slave of Hudhayfah.

The exchange created some ruckus in the Prophet's Mosque. The Caliph immediately came down from the pulpit, grabbed the hand of Umar, and went to his home. They did not leave his house for three days. When the fourth day arrived, it came with a thousand men waiting outside Abu Bakr's home.

Khalid ibn al-Walid, the head of these thousand men, called out to Abu Bakr and Umar from outside the house. "Why do you sit in your homes? By Allah, Bani Hashim have set their eyes upon the caliphate!"

They would peak outside to see another two thousand men assemble with Salim and Ma'adh. Before the end of the day, the group swelled to a total of four thousand men. Umar rejoiced and took the lead of the small army of men. They marched on to the Prophet's Mosque with their swords unsheathed and brought Abu Bakr there to sit back up on the pulpit.

Seeing Ali's men at the Mosque, Umar stared them down cold-eyed. He did not wait too long before calling them out.

"O companions of Ali! By Allah, if anyone among you says what they said yesterday, your heads shall roll…"

Khalid ibn Said immediately stood up and faced Umar.

O son of Sahhak! Do you threaten us with your swords and large numbers? By Allah! Our swords are sharper than yours and we are also greater in sum! We may seem small in numbers; however, we are far more because the 'evidence of Allah' is amongst us. By Allah! If we had not held the obedience of our Imam to be dearer than anything else, we would have unsheathed our swords and fought you until we take our rights from you…

At this time, Imam Ali was also present. Hearing the words of Khalid, he came near him and acknowledged his position.

"Allah has recognized your stand and has reserved a suitable reward for you," he told Khalid. "But now, sit down."

Khalid sat down dutifully. As Khalid sat, Salman would rise and speak.

Allah is Great! Allah is Great! I have heard with my ears from the Prophet of Allah, and may my ears turn deaf if I speak a lie, where he said, 'It shall come forth *that my brother and the son of my uncle, Ali, will be seated in the masjid with a group of his companions, then a group of hellhounds will surround them and resolve to kill them.' I do not doubt that the ones referred to by the Prophet are you who have come to kill Ali and his companions.*

Umar was enraged by the accusation. He could not restrain himself. He leaped towards Salman to attack him; sword unsheathed. Before reaching him, Imam Ali grabbed Umar by his collar, lifted him off the ground and threw him down. As Umar lay there defeated, Ali came in closer and said with a voice as steady as steel.

O son of Sahhak, if the command of Allah had not been written and the promise had not been given to the Prophet regarding this, I would have shown you who among us is weak with regards to companions and less in numbers!

The Twelve Men were ready, their palms gripping the handles of their swords. Ali turned to them and saw their valor. They admired his own and were inspired by it.

Rise and leave my men. May Allah's blessings be upon you! By Allah, I will never enter the Mosque, but like my brothers Prophets Moses and Aaron, when the Children of Israel told them: 'Both of you go with your Lord and fight, indeed we shall stay here sitting.' By Allah, I will not enter the Mosque except to visit the grave of the Prophet of Allah, or to judge by the orders

of Allah, for it is not lawful to delay the command-
ments of Allah that have been brought by the Prophet
of Allah and to leave people in a state of perplexity and
distress.

Still laying on the ground, Umar watched Imam Ali and the
men as they left the Mosque.

Days later, Ali was found in Medina speaking to the people.
He gave his sermon from the Prophet's Mosque. Ali began in
God's glorious name as he always had and sang His praises.

Be aware! I swear upon Allah Who split open the seed
and created mankind, that if you had obtained the
knowledge and excellence from the mine (i.e. the orig-
inal source), and drank the water when it was pure and
agreeable, observed righteousness from its original
place, paved the way through the illuminated path, and
traversed righteousness from its own path; the path of
salvation would have been manifest upon you, the
signs of righteousness would have been apparent and
the customs of Islam would have been illuminated for
you. Then you would have enjoyed the blessings of Al-
lah abundantly, and not a single family from among
you Muslims would have fallen victim to indigence
and oppression, and even the protected disbelievers
would have been in peace.

However, you traversed the path of the tyrants while
your world turned dark even though it was vast. The
doors of knowledge and excellence closed upon your

faces. You then spoke in conformity to the whims of your desires. You created discord in your religion and gave verdict in the religion of Allah without knowing anything. Then you obeyed the astray ones who misled you and you betrayed the 'masters of righteousness,' and they too left you to your own selves!

You dawned under the influences of your whims and then, when you faced a problem, you asked the 'People of the Dhikr'. When we give you our verdict regarding it, you say: 'Knowledge is but here', but then what is the use of this confession to your state when you do not follow them in practice, rather you oppose them and leave their orders behind your backs! Be quiet! Soon you shall reap what you have sown and shall witness the punishment of your deeds.

I swear by Allah Who split open the seed and created the human being, you very well know that I am your leader and guide, and I am the one whose obedience has been assigned. I am the erudite among you under whose light the right path can be paved; I am the vicegerent of your Prophet and the chosen one of your Lord; the tongue of your light; the one cognizant of your affairs. Then very soon shall the wrath of Allah descend upon you regarding what you have been promised, just like it descended upon the people before you. Very soon will Allah ask you regarding your Imam and you will arise along with your Imam and return to your Lord.

I swear by Allah! If I had along with me such quantity of men equaling the men of Talut or similar to the combatants at Badr, and they in turn would be your enemies, I would have struck at you with the sword along with them, until I would have bent you to righteousness and truth. This striking is better for shutting down the path of infidelity and hypocrisy and would be more effective than leniency and moderateness. O Allah! Judge between us with righteousness for surely You are the best Judge.

After he finished his sermon, Ali walked out of the Mosque and into the desert plains. He walked quite a distance and came upon a flock of sheep. There was a little over thirty sheep that had taken shelter in a pen. At this sight Ali proclaimed,

By Allah! If I had with me men who were true supporters of Allah, the Mighty, the Sublime, and His Prophet, equaling the number of these sheep, I would certainly have deposed this one from his authority.

As the day neared its end, Ali went back to the town of Medina. A group of three hundred sixty people came before him and bowed at his humble majesty. They swore allegiance to him and took an oath to protect and defend the Imam until death overcame them. Not giving much of a reaction to the new band of men, Ali nodded and gave them their first task.

"Go now and come back tomorrow to me with shaven heads at the street of Ahjar al-Zait." They responded in the affirmative and promised to see their leader tomorrow.

The next day quickly came. Imam Ali arrived at the street of Ahjar al-Zait with his head shaved. He waited for the three hundred and sixty men to arrive, but there was no trace of them. They did not show at all. Instead, only five men came forth in the manner that the Imam requested. The first amongst them was Abuthar. Al-Miqdad followed him soon after. Hudhayfah ibn al-Yaman then came forth, who was then followed by Ammar. Salman was the final comer of the group. With heads shaven, Ali and his small group of men sat and reflected on their reality.

The Commander of the Faithful raised his hands to the Heavens in supplication.

> O Allah! The community has weakened me similar to the Children of Israel who had weakened Aaron. O Allah! You are well aware of what is hidden in our hearts and what we reveal, while nothing in the Heavens or the Earth is hidden from You. Let me die the death of a Muslim and unite me with the virtuous ones. I swear by the Kaabah and the one who takes to the Kaabah! If there would not have been the promise and testimony of the Prophet, I would have flung the opponents into the canal of perdition and would have sent storms of thunderbolts of death towards them. Then soon would they have understood the meaning of my speech.

It was in these days that Ali would take Lady Fatima to the homes of the Prophet's supporters, the Ansar, and speak of the ordeal they faced. In these visits, Fatima would call onto the Ansar to support Ali as they supported her father Muhammad.

Muawiyah ibn Abi Sufyan was an onlooker during this period. In a time that would come, Muawiyah would scoff at Ali and remind him of this miserly time he endured.

> I cannot help but remember the days when you seated your wife upon a donkey, clasping the hands of your Hasan and Husayn. On that day, people had sworn allegiance to Abu Bakr. You went in pursuit of the people of Badr and those who were foremost in coming to Islam and invited them towards yourself. You, along with your wife and sons, requested them to assist one another in defending your rights and told the men to come and take allegiance at the hands of the defender of the Prophet of Allah, but none, except four or five, accepted your call.
>
> If you had been upon the truth, they would certainly have accepted your call. But your claim was false, and you subconsciously uttered words and aimed at the affair of the caliphate that you had failed to achieve! You have forgotten, while I have not, the words you spoke to Abu Sufyan when he invited you to take the authority in your hands. You said, 'If forty strong and steadfast men were along with me, I would have fought with these men.' But the view of the Muslims is not along with you...

History would tell that this son of Abu Sufyan, the archenemy of the Prophet, would come to challenge Ali and the sons of Fatima in the years ahead. He would ascend the ranks of the caliphs and wage war on Ali when the people chose Ali to lead twenty-five years later. Muawiya would go on to fight the sons of Fatima, after Ali's death, and would not stop until he sat in the seat of the caliphate himself. His son, Yazid, would have the son of Fatima, Husayn, massacred in Karbala.

CHAPTER 10

A LAND CALLED FADAK

Why did you take away the land that my father had left for me and expel my deputy from there when the Prophet had declared it to be my property by the command of Allah?

– Lady Fatima

After Abu Bakr's reign was established in the weeks that had passed, he made sweeping policies that bolstered his new administration. One of those policies was claiming lands for the state, amongst those lands was Fadak. The Caliph ordered that the land of Fadak was to be under the ownership of the state and that the deputy of Fatima who took care of the lands was to be expelled immediately.

The news of the state order came to Fatima. She immediately went to the Caliph and protested the matter without hesitation.

"Why did you take away the land that my father had left for me and expel my deputy from there when the Prophet had declared it to be my property by the command of Allah?"

"Bring me a witness for your claim," he replied. In response, Fatima left and brought Umm Ayman as her witness in the matter.

Before Umm Ayman would give testimony, she made one thing clear to the Caliph.

"I shall not bear witness until I make you, O Abu Bakr, confirm my merits in the words of the Prophet of Allah!"

Taken aback, Abu Bakr nodded awaiting to hear what merits she spoke of.

"I ask you in the name of Allah, did the Prophet not say that verily Umm Ayman is from among the women of paradise?"

"Yes, the Prophet said so," he affirmed.

Umm Ayman confidently continued, "I bear witness that Almighty Allah sent revelation to His Prophet saying: 'And give to the near of kin their due.' When this verse was revealed upon the Prophet, he immediately gifted Fadak to Fatima."

After Umm Ayman's testimony, Imam Ali came forth and gave his own testimony affirming that Fadak belonged to Fatima outright.

The given testimony convinced the Caliph that the lands of Fadak indeed belonged to Lady Fatima. Thus, the Caliph proceeded to write a letter rebuking his previous claim that the property belonged to the state. While this transaction was taking place, Umar caught wind of what was going on. He rushed to the Caliph and saw him handing the letter to Fatima.

"What is this?" he demanded, pointing at the letter.

"Fatima came to me claiming that Fadak was her property, and she brought Umm Ayman and Ali as witnesses for her statement. On this basis I wrote a letter handing Fadak back to Fatima, giving her this letter," the Caliph replied.

Umar snatched the letter from Fatima's hands and tore it to shreds. He puffed his chest and then announced to all those present:

> *Fadak is among the spoils of war, and it belongs to all the Muslims! Malik ibn Aws ibn al-Hadathan, Aishah and Hafsah all bore witness that the Prophet of Allah said, 'We the group of prophets do not leave anything as inheritance, whatever we leave behind is charity.' As for the witness of Ali, he is the husband of Fatima and will thus look after his own wellbeing. As for Umme Ayman, she is a righteous woman and if another person bears witness alongside her, then we will accept this claim.*

Fatima looked at them with hurt in her eyes, not shedding a tear but rather shards of pain. From her childhood to that very moment, never was a moment of her life free from animosity and harm.

"Just as you have ripped this letter of mine, may Allah rip your stomachs," she prayed.

The very next day, Imam Ali went directly to the Caliph where he stood in the Mosque. He was surrounded by scores of men from both the Muhajiroun and the Ansar.

"Why did you forbid Fatima from the inheritance that she received from her father, the Prophet of Allah, which he had handed over to Fatima during his lifetime?" Ali questioned him in front of them all.

"Fadak is from the spoils of war and is associated with all the Muslims. Thus, if Fatima brings witnesses that the Prophet of Allah had given it to her as her own personal property, we will give it to her, otherwise she has no claim over it," Abu Bakr defended.

Imam Ali firmly replied, "O Abu Bakr! You have judged against the orders of Allah regarding us among the Muslims."

"It is not so!" Abu Bakr jolted back.

"If a property is in the possession of another Muslim and is under his control and I was to claim that it is my property, from whom will you ask for two witnesses?"

"I shall ask you to produce two witnesses to support your claim," Abu Bakr responded.

Then why do you ask for two witnesses from Fatima regarding a property that was already under her possession, and it was very much under her possession during the lifetime of the Prophet and even after his death? Why do you not ask the Muslims to produce two witnesses on their claim in the same way that you ask me to produce witnesses when I claim the property under the possession of someone else?

The Caliph could not offer a reply, rather silence overcame him, and he stared blankly back at Ali. Umar barged in and came to Abu Bakr's defense.

"O Ali! Keep aside these talks for we do not have the capacity to refute your claims. If you bring just witnesses, then we will accept your claim. If not, Fadak is the property of all the Muslims, and you and Fatima have no claim to it!"

Ali ignored Umar and spoke again to the Caliph.

He asked him, "Have you read the Qur'an?"

Abu Bakr replied, "Yes."

"Then tell me in whose praise was this verse of the Qur'an revealed, 'Verily Allah intends to keep off from you every kind of uncleanliness, O Ahlulbayt, and purify you a thorough purification.' Is this verse revealed in our praise or anyone else?"

"It is revealed in your praise," Abu Bakr admitted.

"Presume that some people bear witness that Fatima has committed a crime, what would your orders be in her regard?"

"I shall punish her according to the laws of Allah as I would do to any other woman," Abu Bakr replied simply.

Imam Ali responded, "In that case you would be among the disbelievers in the sight of Allah!"

"Why is that?" he asked.

For you would have refuted the witness of Allah regarding the chastity of Fatima and accepted the wit-

ness of the people. Thus, you have rejected the com-
mand of Allah and that of the Prophet of Allah. The
Prophet gifted Fadak to Fatima under the direct com-
mand of Allah and it remained under her possession
in the lifetime of the Prophet. You refute this com-
mand of Allah, and you accept the witness of a Bed-
ouin who urinates upon his heels? You snatch Fadak
away from Fatima and claim that it is from among the
spoils of war for all Muslims, whereas the Prophet of
Allah had said that proof is to be brought by the claim-
ant while an oath is to be taken by the defendant! You
refute the words of the Prophet of Allah!

There was an uproar amongst the people, enraged by the injustice that had now been made so clear to them.

"By Allah, Ali speaks the truth!" they called out.

But nothing changed in those moments. People's cries fell
upon deaf ears, and they were nothing more than calls without
action. Ali returned home.

Fatima went back to mourn over the grave of her father.
Upon his grave she recited, "Verily such silent conspiracies arose
after you, that if you were present, they would not have increased
as they have after you…"

When the Caliph and his right hand retired from the
Mosque, they reflected on what had transpired. They sat down
and looked at each other with serious considerations of what was
to come. Abu Bakr told Umar what was on his mind of qualms
and hesitancies.

"Did you see how the discourse between Ali and myself concluded? If such clashes take place between us again, certainly our power will tremble and the pillars of our authority will become unstable," Abu Bakr said to Umar while Umar rubbed his chin.

When the lands of Fadak were taken away from Lady Fatima by order of the state, the laborers that worked the land were kicked out and told to find work elsewhere. Upon receiving the news of the caliphate's decision, Imam Ali immediately addressed the Caliph both in person and by written letter. In part, Ali's letter stated,

> Steer through the waves of mischief by the boats of deliverance; put off the crowns of pride and turn away from the conceit of egoistic men. You should turn towards the fountainhead of grace and light.

> You have taken for yourself the inheritance left by the 'pure souls.' Now, come out of the circle of ignorance, negligence, and perplexity. It is as if I see with my eyes that you, similar to a blindfolded camel, are circumambulating around destruction and walking in bewilderment and distress. By Allah! If I had been ordered, I would have blown your heads off similar to the ripping of the ready harvest with a sharp iron sickle, and I would have severed the heads of your brave ones with such a ferocity that your eyes would be wounded and each one of you would be frightened and perplexed.

> I am the one who has scattered the abundant crowd of enemies and had destroyed armies and thus, I could

strike at your group and your customs! I was busy in the battlefield fighting the enemies, while you fled back to your homes!

Just yesterday, I was busy in serving the Prophet and all of you were aware of my deeds and acknowledged my status.

I swear by the life of my father! You never did consent that prophethood and caliphate would both be combined in our family. You still have not forgotten the envy of the battles of Badr and Uhud. By Allah! If we reveal to you what Almighty Allah has decreed regarding you, certainly the bones of your ribs would enter your bodies similar to the points of the compass.

If I speak out, they will call me greedy for power, but if I keep quiet, they will say that Ali ibn Abi Talib is afraid of death. Alas! Alas! I am more desirous of death than an infant is to the breast of its mother. I am the one who has made the many enemies taste death and have greeted death with open arms in the battlefield. I do not have the slightest fear or terror of death. I am the one who turned away the flags of the enemies in the pitch-black darkness of the night; I am the one who warded off blockade and sorrow for the sake of the Prophet, and I am authorized to tell you what Allah has revealed regarding you and I know it, and if you were to hear it then you would tremble like ropes in deep wells and would wander in the desert in bewilderment. But I am forbearing and lead a simple and modest life, so that I may meet the Lord of the Universe with hands empty of the pleasures of this life and a heart vacant of darkness.

Know that the reality of this world of yours is similar to the cloud that hangs in the air and looks wide and thick over the heads of men, then it suddenly disappears and scatters away! Very soon will the dust set from in front of your eyes, and you shall witness the results of your evil deeds, and at that point, you will reap the bitter seeds of poison and perdition that you have sown. Know that Allah is the Best Judge and His beloved Prophet will be your greatest enemy, while the ground of the Resurrection will be your place of return.

Allah will keep you away from His mercy and He will engulf you in His severe wrath; and peace will be unto him who follows the guidance.

After he finished reading the letter, the Caliph grew agitated and uneasy. He read the letter in the presence of his men. He rose out of his seat and spoke to those in his midst.

What an astonishment! Indeed, Ali has demonstrated such a show of audacity and boldness against me! O group of Muhajiroun and Ansar! Did I not discuss with you the matter of Fadak? Did you not tell me that the prophets do not leave behind anything as inheritance? Did you not declare that it was necessary that

Fadak should be used to guard and mobilize the frontiers and for the general well-being of the people?

Certainly, I accepted your advice and approved of what you stated, but now Ali ibn Abi Talib opposes this view and threatens me with words similar to the sparks of lightening and the roaring of thunder! He opposes my caliphate. I wish to resign from this; however, you do not permit. From the first day of opposition, I did not want to come face to face with Ali and flee... to this day I avoid confrontation with him.

His closest confidant, Umar, was again outraged by the Caliph's weak responses to Ali's arguments.

Can you not say anything else except such things?! You are the son of that father who was never at the forefront of any battle, nor was he generous and beneficent during the days of severity and famine. Glory be to Allah! What a coward and timid man, possessing a weak heart you are!

I handed you this caliphate as clear and pleasant water, but you are not ready to take benefit from it nor quench your thirst with it? I made the stubborn necks bow and submit to you and gathered diplomats and experienced men around you. If it would not have been for my efforts and endeavor, this success would not have come to you and certainly Ali ibn Abi Talib would have broken your bones!

*Offer thanks to Allah that because of me you have ac-
quired this significant position, when certainly the one
who acquires the place of the Prophet of Allah on his
pulpit should thank Allah. This Ali, the son of Abu
Talib, is similar to a solid rock that cannot break so
that water may pass through it; and he is similar to a
dangerous snake that cannot be tamed except through
charm and trick; and he is similar to a bitter tree that
even if it is fed honey, it will not bear sweet fruit. He
has killed the brave men among the Quraysh and has
crushed the stubborn ones. Be calm and do not fear his
threats and do not let your heart tremble by his light-
ning and thunder. I shall finish his task and stop his
way before he steps forth to hurt you."*

Abu Bakr brushed his companion off and waved him down
with the back of his hand.

*Keep aside these extravagant talks as by Allah, if Ali
wishes he can kill us with his left hand without even
having to use his right. There are three factors in our
favor: first, he is alone and has no aide; second, he is
under compulsion to act according to the testimony of
the Prophet to forebear and he will never go against it;
and third, seeing as how most of the people of the various tribes envy him and bear animosity towards him
because their family, the infidels, had been killed at his
hands – they do not want to establish favorable rela-
tions with him. If these factors would not have been*

there, certainly the caliphate would have gone to him and our opposition would be useless.

O son of al-Khattab! Pay attention that Ali ibn Abi Talib, just like he has written in his letter, is not inclined towards this world and he flees from the life of this world, while we are frightful of death and flee from it, so how will such a man fear death?"

CHAPTER 11

WE ARE WAITING

O' people, know that I am Fatima, and my father is Muhammad.

– Lady Fatima

Lady Fatima could not bear the injustice that had taken place so close after her father's death. She took to the Mosque of the Prophet where the caliph and the people had gathered. In her veil and long gown, she walked the streets of Medina as her father did. She walked tall but with a prophetic humbleness and grace.

Her women gathered around her and followed. About her was a prestige that was beyond royalty, it was heavenly. It was as if the angels of God had marched on to the Mosque of the Prophet to show the people the position of Heaven from the inhabitants of Earth.

As Fatima entered the mosque, a veil was placed to separate her from the people out of respect for her chastity and her honor as the daughter of God's Messenger. Fatima did not speak any words as she entered, she let out only sighs of grief, sighs that told the story of the oppression endured, of the injustices that weaved themselves into her days. Her sighs were so profound that the entire mosque shook in cries and wails. Fatima waited for the cries to quiet down. When they did, The Lady of Light finally spoke with wisdom beyond her years, and with truths that could awaken even the darkest hearts, leaving all witnesses, both human and angel, in contemplation and awe.

> *Praise be to God for that which He bestowed upon us, and thanks be to Him for all that which He inspired, and tribute be to Him for that which He provided; from prevalent favors which He created, and abundant benefactions which He offered and perfect grants which He presented; that their number is much too plentiful to compute, and too vast to measure; their limit was too distant to realize. He recommended to them, His creatures, to gain more of His bounties by being grateful for their continuity. He ordained Himself praiseworthy by giving generously to His creatures, and promised, through supplicating Him, to give more like them.*

> *I bear witness that there is no God but God who is one without a partner; a statement which sincere devotion is made to be its interpretation, put into hearts its continuation, and illuminated in the minds its sensibility. He who cannot be perceived with vision, neither be described with tongues, nor can imagination surround His form.*

> *He originated things but not from anything that existed before them and created them without examples to follow. He created them with His might and dispersed them according to His will; not for a need did*

He create them, nor for a benefit for Him did He shape them, but to establish His wisdom, bring attention to His obedience, manifest His might, lead His creatures to humbly venerate Him, and to exalt His decrees. He then made the reward for His obedience, and punishment for His disobedience, so as to protect His creatures from His wrath and amass them into His Paradise.

I too bear witness that my father, Muhammad, is His slave and messenger, whom He chose before sending him, named him before creating him, and preferred him by missioning him; when creatures were still concealed in the unseen, guarded from that which was appalling, and associated with the termination and nonexistence. For God the Exalted knew that which was to follow, comprehended that which will come to pass, and realized the place of every event. God has sent him as perfection for His commands, a resolution to accomplish His rule, and an implementation of His decrees.

So, he found the nations to vary in their faiths, obsessed by their fires, worshipping their idols, and denying God despite their knowledge of Him. Therefore, God illuminated their darkness with my father, Muhammad, uncovered obscurity from their hearts and cleared the clouds from their insights. He revealed guidance among the people. He delivered them from being led astray, led them away from misguidance, *guided them to the proper religion, and called them to the straight path.*

Allah then chose to recall him back in mercy, love, and preference. So, Muhammad is in comfort from the burden of this world, he is surrounded with devoted angels, the satisfaction of the Merciful Lord, and the nearness of the Powerful King.

May the blessing of God be upon my father, His Prophet, the trusted one with the revelation, the choice from among His creatures, and His sincere friend. May the peace and blessings of God be upon him.

Lady Fatima paused and then turned back to her audience that did not move an inch from their seats. It was much to take in, as the daughter of the Prophet spoke with the eloquence of her father. She continued.

You are God's slaves at His command and prohibition. You are the bearers of His religion and revelation. You are God's trusted ones with yourselves, and His messengers to the nations. Among you He has a right; a covenant He brought unto you, and an heir He left over you. That is the eloquent Book of God, the truthful Quran, the brilliant light, and the shining beam. Its insights are clear, its secrets are revealed, its indications are manifest, and its followers are blessed by it. It leads its adherents to bliss and listening to it leads to salvation. With it are the bright divine authorities achieved, His manifest determination acquired, His prohibited decrees avoided, His manifest evidence recognized, His satisfying proofs made apparent, His permissions granted, and His written laws are achieved.

God made faith to be a purification for you from polytheism. He made prayer an exaltation for you from conceit, zakat a purification for the soul and a cause of growth in subsistence, fasting an implantation of devotion, pilgrimage a construction of religion, justice a harmony of the hearts, obeying us, Ahlulbayt, management of the nation, our leadership safeguard from disunity, struggle in strengthening of Islam, patience a helping course for deserving divine reward, enjoining the good welfare for the public, kindness to the parents a safeguard from wrath, maintaining kinship a cause for a longer life and multiplying the number of descendants, retaliation for sparing blood, fulfillment of vows deserving of forgiveness, completion of weights and measures preventing from ignoring others' rights, forbiddance of drinking wines an exaltation from atrocity, avoiding slander a veil from curse, abandoning theft a reason for deserving chastity.

Allah has also prohibited polytheism so that one can devote himself to His Lordship. Therefore, fear God as He should be feared and die not except that you are Muslims.

Obey God in that which He has commanded you to do and that which He has forbidden you from, for surely those who fear God among His servants are those who have knowledge.

Lady Fatima then said with a veracity and strength that could not be presumed by anyone else.

O' people, know that I am Fatima, and my father is Muhammad. I say that repeatedly and initiate it continually. I say not what I say mistakenly, nor do I do what I do aimlessly.

'Now hath come unto you an Apostle from amongst yourselves. It grieves him that you should perish; ardently anxious is he over you, to the believers he is most kind and merciful.' (9:128)

Thus, if you identify and recognize him, you shall realize that he is my father and not the father of any of your women; the brother of my cousin Ali rather than any of your men. What an excellent assistant to him Ali was, may the peace and blessings of God be upon him and his progeny. Thus, he propagated the Message, by announcing openly with the warning, and inclining away from the path of the polytheists, striking their middles, and seizing their throats, inviting to the way of his Lord with wisdom and good preaching.

He destroyed the idols, broke the heads until their gathering fled and turned their backs, until the night revealed its morning, the truth appeared with its genuineness. The leader of the religion spoke out and the discords of devils were silenced, the stuff of hypocrisy was perished, and the knots of infidelity and desertion were untied. So, you spoke the word of devotion among a group of the white starving ones, the Ahlulbayt.

You were on the brink of a pit of fire, the drink of the thirsty one, the opportunity of the desiring one, the firebrand of a hasty passer… you used to drink from the rainwater gathered on the road and in which animals used to drink and eat animal skin. You were low and despised and always in fear lest men around should extirpate you, but God the Almighty rescued you through my father, Muhammad, peace be upon him and his progeny after much suffering he faced, and after he was confronted by mighty men, the Arab beasts and the insolent, mutinous men of the people of the Book.

Whenever they ignited the fire of war, God extinguished it, and whenever the thorn of the devil appeared, or one of the polytheists opened his mouth in defiance, he would send his brother Ali into its flames. He did not come back until he trod its head with the sole of his foot and extinguished its flames with his sword. He tired himself for the sake of God and overworked to fulfill the command of God. He was near to the Messenger of God, a master among God's devotees, sincere in his advice, earnest and exerting himself for Islam, paying no attention, in the way of God, to *any blame, while you were at ease, in luxury, and feeling safe in your comfortable lives.*

You waited for us to meet disasters, awaiting the spread of our news, and you fell back during battles and ran away at times from fighting. And when God chose for His Prophet the abode of His prophets, and the residence of His choices, the rage of hypocrisy showed on you. The garment of faith became worn out, the silent one of the deviants spoke out, and the sluggish ignorant came to the top and brayed. The camel of the falsifiers wiggled his tail in your courtyards and Satan put his head out of his socket crying out too. He found you responsive to his invitation and observing his deceitful ways.

He then aroused you and found you quick in responding to him. He invited you to anger and found you angry. Therefore, you branded other than your camels and proceeded to other than your drinking places. You did so and the demise of the Prophet was still recent, the wound was still wide and not yet healed, and the Prophet had yet to be buried. Did you so quickly claim the fear of sedition? Surely into sedition have they already tumbled down, and most surely hell encompasses the unbelievers.

What is the matter with you and what a falsehood! God's Book is still among you, its affairs are clear, its rules are manifest, its signs are bright, its restrictions are visible, and its commands are evident. Yet indeed you have thrown it behind your backs! Do you want to turn away from it? Or according to something else you want to rule? Evil would be the exchange for the wrongdoers! And if anyone desires a religion other than Islam, it will never be accepted from him, and in the hereafter, he will be in the ranks of those who have lost.

Then you have not waited until its rush would calm down, and it became obedient. You then began arousing its flames, instigating its brand, responding to the call of the misguiding Satan, putting out the lights of the manifest religion, and annulling the tradition of the sincere Prophet. You conceal sips on foam and march towards the Prophet's family and children in thickets and forests, but we are patient with you as if we are being nicked with daggers and stung by spearheads in our abdomens, and now you claim that there is no inheritance for us!

'Is it then the judgment of the times of ignorance that they desire? And who is better than God to judge for a people who are sure?' (5:50)

Do you not know? Yes, indeed it is obvious to you like the sun of the forenoon that I am his daughter.

O' Muslims, is my inheritance usurped? O' son of Abu Quhafa, is it in the Book of God that you inherit your father and I do not inherit my father? Surely you have done a strange thing! Did you intendedly desert the Book of God and turned your back on it?

Allah said, 'And Sulaiman was Dawood's heir' (27:16). And said about Yahya bin Zachariah, 'Grant me from thyself an heir, who should inherit me and inherit from the children of Jacob' (19:5-6). And said, 'And the possessors of relationships are nearer to each other in the ordinance of God' (8:75). And He said, 'Allah enjoins you concerning your children: the male shall have the equal of the portion of two females' (4:11). God said, 'Bequest is prescribed for you when death approaches one of you if he leaves behind wealth for parents and near relatives' (2:180).

You claimed that I have no position, and no inheritance from my father, and there is no kinship between us. So did God distinguish you with a verse, from which He excluded my father? Or do you say: people of two religions do not inherit each other? Am I and my father not of one religion? Or are you more aware of the Quran than my father and my cousin?

So, here it is before you! Take it with its noseband and saddle. It shall dispute with you on the Day of Punishment; what a fair judge God is, the master is Muhammad, and the appointment is the Day of Resurrection. At the time of the Hour the wrongdoers shall lose, and it shall not benefit you to regret then! For every Message, there is a time limit, and you shall know to whom a punishment that will confound him comes, and upon whom a lasting doom will fall.

Lady Fatima then turned to the Ansar in the crowd and addressed them point blank.

O' you people of magnanimity, the supporters of the nation, and the defenders of Islam, what is this shortcoming in defending my rights? And what is slumber before the wrong done to me? Did not the Messenger of God, my father, say: 'A man is observed through his children'? How quick have you violated and how soon have you let down? Though you are still are able to help me in my attempt and assist in what I request.

Do you say: 'Muhammad has died'? Surely, this is a great calamity that its damage is great, its injury is wide, and its wound is much torn. The earth became dark with his departure, the sun and the moon eclipsed, the stars scattered for his calamity, hopes were skimped, mountains submitted, sanctity was violated, and holiness was encroached after his death. This, by God, is the great affliction, and the impressive calamity that there is no suffering, nor is there a sudden misfortune like it. The Book of God, the most praised, announced in your courtyards, in your evening and mornings in calling, crying, recitation, and intonation; and before him what had happened to the prophets and messengers of God; a final decree, and a determined predestination:

'Muhammad is not but an Apostle; many were the apostles that passed away before him. If he died or was killed, will you then turn back on your heels? If any did turn back on his heels, not the least harm will he do to God; but God will reward those who are grateful.' (3:144).

O' people of Qaylah (the tribes of Aous and Khazraj), is the inheritance of my father usurped while you hear and see me?! And you are in your meetings and gatherings around me? You hear my call, and the affair includes you though you are numerous and well equipped with power and good shield?! The call reaches you, but you do not respond, and the cry comes to you, but you do not help. You do this while you are qualified by struggle, known for goodness and welfare, and are the choice that were chosen, and the best selection that were selected for us, Ahlulbayt.

You fought the Arabs, bore tire and exhaustion, struggled against the nations, and resisted their mutinous ones. We were still. We ordered you and you obeyed, until when Islam became triumphant, the accomplishment of the days was at hand, the nose of polytheism was subjected, the outburst of falsehood was calmed, the fires of infidelity were put out, the call of commotion was quelled, and the system of religion was well-ordered. Then why have you become confused after lucidity, concealed after the openness, receded after daring, and polytheists after faith?

'Will you not fight a people who broke their oaths and aimed at expelling the Messenger, and they attacked you first; do you fear them? But God is most deserving that you should fear Him, if you are believers.' (9:13).

Surely, I see that you have inclined to ease, dismissed one who is worthier of giving and preventing, secluded yourselves with easiness, escaped from narrowness to abundance, so you spat out what you had contained, and vomited what you had drank. 'If you are ungrateful, you and those on earth all together, most surely God is self-sufficient, praised.'

Indeed, I have said all that which I said with knowing of the disappointment that preoccupied you, and the betrayal that your hearts felt... And so here it is. Carry it on the back of a camel, which has a thin slipper, with everlasting disgrace, marked with the wrath of God, and eternal dishonor, attached to the burning Fire of God, which rises above the hearts. It is in the eye of God that which you do 'and those who do wrong will come to know by what a great reverse they will be overturned!' And I am the daughter of a warner to you against a severe punishment. 'So, act and we are acting. And wait, and we are waiting.'" (11:121-122)

Those were the eternal words of Fatima, laced with the Word of God. For how could the Lady of Light speak, without speaking the Truth that came from her Lord? Nothing came from her home but revelation. But did the people heed to the Word? Did they realize that they were in the midst of God's most honored ambassadors? Or were they blind to even the most radiating Truth?

CHAPTER 12

YOUR WORLD AND YOUR MEN

By God, I shall not permit them, nor even utter a word with them until I meet my father the Prophet of God, and I will complain to him about their treatment of me.

– Lady Fatima

Fatima would grow ill from her injuries. Her body could not recover from the wounds she sustained when her home was attacked by the Caliph's men. A group of women from the community would visit her in her illness. They entered the house of Fatima and tried to console her with their presence. They asked, "How are you doing, daughter of God's Messenger?"

Fatima would turn to them. The pain she displayed was beyond any physical agony. The pain of Fatima was that of the heart, the mind, and the soul. The oppression she endured was so unique, it could not be matched by any other human experience. In her pain, she looked towards them with eyes that gazed beyond this lowly world. In her pain, she replied.

By God, I have come to resent your world and detest your men. I have cast them away after testing them and despised them after examining them. Thus, away with the men of playing after seriousness, striking the soft

rocks, slackening the spears, the foolishness of judg-
ments, and deviation of fancies!

'Certainly, evil is that which their souls have sent be-
fore for them, that God became displeased with them
and in chastisement shall they abide.' (5:80).

Indeed, I have girted them with its noose, burdened
them with its load, and waged its raid on them. So, may
the unjust people be killed, cursed, and damned.

Woe unto them! Whereto did they move it from the
position of the mission, the bases of the prophethood
and the place of descent of Gabriel, who is aware of the
affairs of life and religion? That was the great loss.
What did they deny from Abul-Hasan Ali? Yes, they
denied the beating of his sword, his disregard of his
own death, his deadly assaults, and his anger for the
sake of God.

By God, if they turned away from the reign, which the
Prophet had handed over to him he would catch it ten-
derly and he would move without harm or worry. He
would lead them to a fresh flowing fountain and would
return them with satiety while he himself would not
profit of anything but a little, just to break his acute
thirst and hunger. If they did so, they would be granted
blessings from the Heaven and the earth, and they
would be rewarded by God according to their deeds.

Come on to see! As long as you live, time shall show
you wonders! I wish I knew on what proof they have

relied, to what refuge they resorted and to what tie they clung, and on whose progeny have they encroached and spoke against! Evil indeed is the patron, and evil indeed is the associate, and evil indeed is this change for the unjust! By God, they exchanged the good with the bad and the daring with the impotent. Disgrace be for a people, who think they do well. Surely, they themselves are the mischief makers, but they do not perceive. Woe to them!

'Is he then who guides to the truth more worthy to be followed, or he who himself does not go aright unless he is guided? What then is the matter with you; how do you judge?' (10:35).

By God, it was impregnated so wait until it bears, then milk pure blood and fatal venom to the full of the bucket! Then they will perish who say false things and the successors will know what evil the earlier ones have established. Then, be at ease and wait relatedly for the sedition. Rejoice at a sharp sword, an assault of a tyrant enemy, general commotion, and despotism, which will make your victuals so insignificant, and your gatherings separate.

Alas, what a pity! How will you be while it has been obscured to your sights? Shall we then force you to accept it when you are averse to it?

And praise be to God, the Lord of the worlds, and blessings be on Muhammad, the last of the prophets and the master of the messengers.

As the days passed, Lady Fatima only grew more and more ill. She asked her husband to keep her condition private, as she did not want certain individuals to visit her or know about her situation. He, of course, complied and met every one of her wishes.

Nevertheless, the Caliph and his men would come to know of Fatima's illness. They desired to visit her in her home. Knocking on her door, they asked permission to enter. When Fatima was told who waited on her door to see her, she refused to let them in. Lady Fatima was not eager for such company, nor for excuses to salt the wounds. She was satisfied with the presence of God's angels and disciples. As her condition worsened, God had sent her the company of Lady Mary and a fleet of heavenly maidens. It was not the first time that Lady Fatima would receive such company from the Gardens of Paradise.

After being refused, Umar hesitantly beseeched Ali asking him to intercede on their behalf. The Caliph sincerely wished to see Fatima and if anyone could convince her it would be her beloved Ali. Umar asked Ali,

Indeed, Abu Bakr is an old man with a soft heart, he is the one who accompanied the Prophet in the cave and is among his companions. I came here many times with him and asked permission to enter, however, Fat-

ima refused to see us. If you deem it right, take permission for us from Fatima so that we may come and visit her.

Ali went by the bedside of Fatima and delicately held her hand as he always had.

O daughter of God's Prophet, you know that these two men have requested to come to your presence many times and you refused them. They have come once more, asking me to request your permission to visit you.

Fatima replied, "By God, I shall not permit them, nor even utter a word with them until I meet my father the Prophet of God, and I will complain to him about their treatment of me."

"I have assured them that I shall seek permission," Ali replied softly. "If you have assured them, then the house is your house… wives are to obey their husbands, and I will not disobey you in anything. You may permit whomsoever you desire."

Ali gave her a look of reassurance and Fatima always trusted his judgment. He went back outside and gestured for the men to come inside. They entered the home after Ali and when they came in, they extended their greetings to Lady Fatima. She did not reply to them. Instead, she turned away her face.

They tried once more to greet her and have her glance at them, but each time she refused to look at them or give them the satisfaction of seeing her. Pain is only inflicted deeper that while the living still breathe, besides passive pity, no action of worth to heal hearts or alleviate suffering arrives.

"Cover my face with another layer of clothing," she asked Ali emphasizing that she did not want them to see her. Acknowledging her dissatisfaction with them, they asked for her forgiveness.

She did not give it to them. Fatima asked the two men.

> I ask you in the Name of Allah, do you remember the day my father, the Prophet of Allah, had asked you to come to visit him at midnight regarding what would come forth for Ali?"

"Yes, we remember," they replied.

> I ask you in the Name of Allah, did you not hear the Prophet say, 'Fatima is from me, and I am from her, the one who hurts her hurts me, and the one who hurts me hurts Allah! And that the one who hurts her after my death is the same as the one who hurt her when I am alive, and the one who hurts her during my lifetime is the same as one who hurt her after my death?'

Again, they replied in the affirmative nodding their heads.

Fatima then lifted her hands to the Heavens and passionately prayed,

> O Lord! These two men have hurt me, I complain of them in Your audience and that of Your Prophet! By Allah! I will not forgive you two nor will I speak to you until I meet my father the Prophet of Allah!

The Caliph buried his face into his hands and cried. He left his place and made his way to the doors crying hysterically.

"Woe is me! The retribution that awaits me! I wish my mother had not given birth to me!"

As he had in previous days, Umar reprimanded the Caliph for his apparent weakness in the presence of others.

> *I wonder how men chose you to lead! You are an old and feeble man that turns restless upon the rage of a woman and rejoices at her pleasure. Spare me from the nonsense of women!*

As they made their way out the door, Fatima called out to them, and they turned.

"Know that I will pray against you in every prayer I pray," Fatima promised.

They lowered their heads and left.

Fatima then turned to Ali and asked, "Now did I fulfil your request?"

Imam Ali replied in the affirmative after which Fatima said, "Now if I desire anything from you, will you do it?"

"Of course," Ali replied to his beloved.

"I request you in the Name of Allah, do something that these two men may not pray upon me after my death and not even stand near my grave."

With her palm in his hand, he reassured her that her wishes would be met. Lady Fatima's crown was her modesty – a divine gift and protection from her Lord, and she guarded it with all her essence, even after her death. Reflecting on the imminent days ahead, she shared her concern with Asma.

> *I do not like how they carry the corpse of women; they place a cloth upon their bier and their body is visible from underneath it. Whoever sees it, knows that it is the body of a man or a woman. I have turned feeble, and the flesh of my body has melted... will you not make something to conceal my body?*

Asma nodded her head in the affirmative.

"When I was in Abyssinia, the people had a bier that would conceal the body, if you desire, I shall make it for you," she told her Lady.

"Make it for me," Fatima replied simply and gratefully.

Asma brought some materials to show Lady Fatima how the bier would look. She placed the plank down on the floor, then affixed some palm-tree wood to its sides. Finally, Asma laid a long piece of cloth on the very top of the bier.

"This is what it looks like my Lady," Asma said as she finished laying out the cloth.

Lady Fatima was pleased with Asma's work, and for the first time after her father's death, she smiled.

"May Allah save you from the fire of hell. Make a similar kind for me and conceal me in it," she told Asma.

Her final days came near. Fatima called for Imam Ali, Umm Ayman, and Asma. They all gathered at her bedside, awaiting her requests. Her eyes fell upon them with her warmth and grace, and she lifted her head to speak. Turning to her beloved Ali she said,

"O Ali, news of my impending death has reached me, and I perceive that I will meet my father very soon. I will to you whatever is in my heart."

"O daughter of the Prophet of God, you may will whatever you desire," Ali replied. He came in closer to her and then turned to everyone else that was present.

"You may be excused," Ali softly told them.

After they left, Fatima gazed at her beloved and shared what was deep within her heart. "O Ali, all throughout my life with you, you have never heard falsehood or seen betrayal from me, nor have I ever disobeyed you," she said with her tender voice.

"No, never," Ali replied keenly. He looked into her eyes and she looked back, both longing for solace. Though the anguish in his eyes said all that was needed to be said, he shared some words from his aching heart.

> You are more learnt, virtuous, pious, and honorable than anyone else... Your separation is unbearable, but there is no escape from death. By Allah, you have renewed the sorrow of the separation from the Prophet and your parting is very hard for me. But indeed, we are for God and to Him we shall return... This is a calamity that has no comfort and is so grave that there is no relief from it.

Ali and Fatima embraced one another and wept for what may have been hours. He held her head to his chest, coddling her with his gracious, breaking heart.

"You may will whatever you desire, certainly you will find me such that I shall fulfil your desire with goodness and endear your behest upon that of mine," he told his beloved.

She wiped away her tears and looked up at Ali. "When I pass away, I want you to give me the ceremonial bath. Shroud me, pray upon me, and bury me. Build my grave and sprinkle earth upon it, then sit at the head of my grave opposite my face and recite the Qur'an abundantly and supplicate, for it is at that moment when a dead person requires affection of the living ones, and I entrust you to Allah and request you to deal with fairness towards my children."

Ali reassured her of his devotion to their children until his last breath. But she continued to weep. Ali embraced her once again and asked her of her tears.

"Why do you weep my dear?"

"I weep upon the sufferings and persecutions that will befall you after me," she replied choked up by her tears.

"Do not weep for me. By God, all these sufferings are nothing for me in the way of God."

If the injustices of her time were not enough to shatter a heart, looking at the distraught face of Ali certainly made sure of it. But she couldn't help herself. Tears over the immaculate beloved were ordained by the Heavens. She continued with her dying wishes to her prince.

"And when I pass away from this world, do not inform anyone except Umm Salma, Umm Ayman and Fiddha, and my children. Among the men, tell our uncle Abbas ibn Abdulmuttalib, Salman, Miqdad, Abuthar and Hudhayfah. I make it lawful for you only to see me after my death, then you may bathe me with the help of the women I mentioned... Bury me in the night and do not inform anyone so that they do not come to my grave."

Ali again promised her that her wishes would be fulfilled without a shadow of doubt. He was her Ali.

Abbas ibn Abdulmuttalib, Lady Fatima's great uncle, wished to see his niece after learning of how bad her state had gotten. He was told that no one was permitted to visit her at that point. Respecting the family's wishes, he left, but decided to send a message to his nephew Imam Ali, carried by one of the companions – Ammar ibn Yasser.

Ammar delivered the message promptly to his Imam.

"O nephew, your uncle sends you greetings... By Allah, this illness of the beloved of the Prophet, the light of his eyes and the light of my eyes – Fatima – has aggrieved me to such an extent, that my life is crushed. I perceive that she will be the first one among us to join the Prophet. I am sure he has chosen for her the best position of paradise and will take her to the presence of Almighty Allah.

"If you perceive that Fatima has passed away, permit me tomorrow to gather the Muhajiroun and Ansar to take part in her funeral proceedings and attend the prayers upon her and thus they may be rewarded for it, for this task is better for the grandeur of Islam."

Imam Ali thanked Ammar for delivering his uncle's message. "Convey my greetings to my uncle Abbas, and give him the following message," Ali replied.

"May Allah not lessen your love for us. I understand your suggestion and your view is fair. But you know that they have oppressed Fatima and usurped her rights and repressed her inheritance that she received from her father, and that they did not honor the recommendations of the Prophet regarding her nor did they consider the rights of Allah. Allah is sufficient as a Judge, and He will exact revenge from the oppressors."

Ali's message ended with the following request, "Dear uncle, I seek apology from you and ask that you excuse me from neglecting your suggestion, for Fatima has willed that I should keep her death a secret."

So it was written, with the dark skies and lit stars as witnesses, that even in her death, Fatima would take a stand against oppression. That in her departure from earth back to the Heavens, in the quiet of night, her silent funeral was to be a revolution against injustice.

CHAPTER 13

BURY ME IN THE NIGHT

O Umm Kulthum! O Zaynab! O Hasan and O Husayn! Come and behold your mother for the time of separation has come.

– Imam Ali

As her final moments came near, Lady Fatima's state of pain began to ease into a heavenly peace. Only a few were in her midst as the angels descended upon her. Fatima's eyes grew wide, and a smile overcame her immaculate face.

"Peace be upon Gabriel! Peace be upon the Prophet of Allah! O Lord, I am accompanying Your Prophet! O Lord! I will be in Your garden and in Your audience, in Your abode, the Abode of Peace," Fatima called out to the Heavens.

She then spoke to the mortals amongst her.

"Do you see what I see?" she asked.

"O daughter of God's Prophet, what do you see?"

"I see the dwellers of the Heavens along with their procession and forms… I see the Angel Gabriel and I see the Prophet of Allah who tells me, 'O daughter! Come to us, for whatever has been reserved for you is the best.'"

Those present were not sure whether to smile or cry. They swam in a limbo of sadness for her departure, and joy for her relief. Fatima asked for solitude in her final moments. They left the room, but Fatima was not left alone. The angels of Heaven continued to descend upon her.

Fatima had asked of Asma to wait for some time before coming back into her room. She told Asma to call out for her after that time, and if she did not reply she should know that she had reunited with her father. Asma complied and waited. In that time, she prepared some food for Fatima's beloved children, doing what she can to ease their pain and console their little hearts.

Anxious to check on Lady Fatima, Asma finally called out and awaited a reply. The reply did not come.

"O daughter of the Chosen One, O daughter of the most Generous One, O daughter of the Immaculate One!"

Asma paused. The silence was stark. No response.

She walked into the room slowly. Opening the door, she found dear Fatima's still body. She summoned whatever strength she found within as she uncovered her face and kissed her forehead.

"O Fatima! When you reach the presence of your father, the Prophet of Allah, convey my greetings to him," Asma whispered as tears flowed down her cheeks.

She walked out of the room, her face pale white. The children came into the house wanting to see their mother.

"Come sit and have your dinner my children," she said blankly. The anguish within was deep, knowing that in moments, she would have to deliver the most painful news that no child should bear. Losing a mother was devasting enough... Yet losing a mother who was the Lady of Light...

"Where is our mother? You know we never eat without her, Asma," they replied.

Asma remained silent, unable to deliver the news to Fatima's precious children.

Hasan and Husayn looked at each other and realized what had happened. They ran to their mother's room and found her lifeless body at the center of it. The boys threw themselves upon their mother's body, embracing her with their little arms.

Hasan kissed her face and forehead and hugged her for dear life. His tears flowed like the Euphrates.

"O mother! Speak to me before my spirit leaves my body. Please speak to me!"

Husayn kissed his mother's feet and sobbed.

"Mother, I am your son Husayn. Please speak to me before my heart is shattered and I die."

Asma was right behind them, crying uncontrollably as she watched these young boys bewail their dead mother.

Asma wiped away her tears and told Hasan and Husayn to go deliver the news to their father Ali. They left the house and made their way to the Prophet's Mosque where their father was praying. Tears glazed their grief-stricken eyes as they walked up to their father.

"What's wrong my sons?" Ali asked as he embraced his young boys.

They looked at him with those eyes and he immediately knew. Ali picked up his sons and ran back to the house. With his sons in his arms, Ali entered Fatima's room. He found Asma at her bedside weeping. She lifted her head up and saw on Ali's face the grief of a breaking heart. Her cries did not relent as she shared in their sorrow.

"O orphans of Muhammad! We were consoling ourselves with Fatima after the passing away of the Prophet, but now who can we find solace with?" she called out.

Imam Ali was struck with such grief that he could not stop weeping. He was restless. His tears were relentless. In those moments, he poetically expressed the loneliness he felt in his shattered heart after his beloved Fatima.

"For every companion there is untimely separation, and every sorrow is forbearing after death; the departure of Fatima after that of Ahmad, proves that for me there is no companion left..."

Imam Ali would put his sons down and take heavy steps toward the body of his beloved. He uncovered her blessed face and touched her cheek and neck. In that, he would find a letter placed behind her head. He delicately unfolded the letter and found Fatima's handwriting.

"In the Name of Allah, the Beneficent, the Merciful… This is the will of Fatima, the daughter of the Prophet of Allah. Fatima bears witness that there is no other deity worthy of worship except Allah and that Muhammad is the Messenger of Allah; paradise and hell are truth and there is no doubt regarding the arrival of the resurrection, and Allah will raise the dead ones from their graves.

"O Ali! I am Fatima, the daughter of Muhammad, whom Allah had united in marriage with you so that I may be linked to you in this world as well as in the hereafter, while you are more worthy of me than anyone else. Give me the ceremonial bath, shroud me, and give me the hunut at night. Then recite prayers upon me and bury me at night, and do not inform anyone else."

Ali read this letter and wept. Moments later, the women of their tribe had gathered outside the house having heard the news of Fatima's death from the family. They joined in the wailing and crying over the loss of Fatima, their source of warmth and light.

"O master of women! O daughter of the Prophet of Allah!" they called out.

Ali with his heavy heart slowly sat down, his sons grasping on to him and sobbing on his shoulders, while his daughters Zaynab and Umm Kulthum remained at their mother's side. Her daughters cried tragically over her, a heart wrenching scene for Asma. The family members paid their respects to Ali. They waited for Fatima's bier to be brought out so that they could pray over her the ritual prayer after death.

In those moments, Ali sent his companion Abuthar to calmly ask the people to give them the solitude to mourn.

Abuthar went outside and announced, "You may leave, for the funeral of Fatima has been postponed until the night."

Nightfall came. As willed by Fatima, Ali would wash the body of his beloved. The only individuals present, as requested by Fatima, were her children Hasan, Husayn, Zaynab, Umme Kulthum, and her dearest companions Fiddha and Asma.

"Fatima had willed that no one should perform the ceremonial washing of her body except Ali and myself, and I assisted him in doing so."

When Ali washed Fatima's body, he prayed to God.

"O Lord! Fatima is Your servant and the daughter of Your Prophet and chosen one. O Lord! Inspire her with her evidences and increase her reasoning, elevate her position and unite her along with her father."

Ali washed and wiped down the body of Fatima with the same cloth he used to wipe the body of the Holy Prophet. As he finished the washing, he gently placed Fatima's body in the bier. He turned to his son Hasan and told him,

"Tell Abuthar and the rest to come here."

The people of Medina were in a deep slumber. The night grew quieter, and the sky went darker. Ammar, Miqdad, Aqeel, Abuthar, Salman and a few men from the Tribe of Hashem followed. As they gathered for the ritual prayer, Ali called out to his children.

"O Umm Kulthum! O Zaynab! O Hasan and O Husayn! Come and behold your mother for the time of separation has come."

They prayed over her blessed soul in her humble home. Their prayers were quiet like the night. Somber recitations filled the air along with the whimpering of children, the cries of women, and the tears of men.

The small band of family and selected companions brought out the bier of Fatima and carried her out in the middle of the night. They walked to the Baqee' Cemetery in a quiet march. Upon arrival they began digging graves, not one but forty. Lady Fatima did not want the place of her grave to be known, and Imam Ali made sure of it.

When Ali finally finished preparing her grave, he lowered her sacred body beneath the earth. As he placed her with his two hands, he recited over his tears.

> *In the Name of Allah, the Beneficent, the Merciful. In the Name of Allah and by Allah, and upon the nation of the Prophet of Allah, Muhammad ibn Abdullah! O Fatima! O Truthful One! I submit you to the One who is better than me and am pleased with what Allah has chosen for you. From the Earth We created you, and into it will We return you.*

The family's cries did not subside and intensified when Ali began to shovel the piles of earth over the body of his beloved. Ali smoothed the dirt over her grave and made it level. As he dusted his hands from the dirt, tears rolled down his cheeks. His grief could not be buried in the soil along with his beloved. It hovered above Fatima's grave and lingered in Medina's dark night.

Ali turned with his sorrow towards the grave of the Prophet. He paused for a moment and took a deep breath. His monologue of grief echoed against the backdrop of the sky's dark canvas.

Peace be upon you O Prophet of Allah, from myself and your daughter that has been laid to rest in your vicinity... She has come back to be quickly reunited with you. My patience has parted away with the separation of your daughter and my strength has faded. However, after facing the heart-rending grief of your separation, all sorrows that reach me are less... I cannot forget the moment when I laid your sacred body into the grave with my own hands, and at the time of death your head was lying on my chest and your sacred soul parted. Indeed, we belong to Allah and indeed we will return back to Him.

O Prophet, the trust that you had bestowed upon me has been returned to you, but my sorrow is undying. I will spend my nights in sleepless sorrow until I too am reunited with you. Very soon your daughter will relate to you how the nation united to oppress us, and you may ask her how this had happened so short after your passing such that your memory had not yet been forgotten.

Salutations upon you both, a farewell salutation – not from weariness or seeking respite. If I leave the site of your grave, it is not that I have grown tired. And if I remain at your grave, it is not that I lack faith in God's promise to the forbearing. Verily patience is more auspicious and fairer. If I had not feared the prevailing of those who have gained power upon us, I would have stayed near your grave and would have performed the spiritual sojourn near your tomb. Then I would raise a sorrowful cry like that of a mother who has lost her son.

Allah is witness that I have buried your daughter in secret fearing the enemies – the daughter whose rights had been usurped and whose inheritance was kept from her shortly after you passed. Your memory had not yet faded... I complain in your presence, O Prophet of Allah, and in your obedience lies consolation of the heart, patience, and fair fortitude. Allah's benediction, blessings and abundance be upon you and your daughter...

Ali sprinkled some more water upon Fatima's grave, and sat down beside the grave with intense grief, weeping. Abbas ibn Abdulmuttalib came forward, and taking hold of Ali's hand, took him home.

That night, forty false graves were made by Ali and his men in the Baqee Cemetery. Scores of people would hear of the news of Fatima's death the next morning and make their way to the cemetery. The site of the forty graves disoriented them. The women began wailing in the agony of not knowing the grave of their Lady Fatima. They looked towards one another for any answers or clues but were left disavowed.

"The Prophet did not leave among you except one daughter, and she passed away from the world and was buried. You could not participate in her burial and funeral, nor can you recognize her grave!" they agonized their cursed state.

Some of the elders tried to calm the people's cries. They said, "Go and bring some believing women that they may come and unearth these graves so that we may find the grave of Fatima."

They looked towards the elders in disbelief, but simultaneously saw it with a glimmer of hope for redemption.

"We may then pray upon her and visit her grave," the elders reassured the people.

As Ali was grieving with his children in the home of Fatima, one of the companions rushed to Ali, and told him the plans of the elders.

Ali immediately leaped out of his seat. His sorrow turned to rage. He grabbed his yellow cloak and dressed it around his shoulders. The last time Ali was seen wearing such a cloak was in battle. The companions watched this lion as a fierce spark gleamed in his eyes and his veins bulged. Ali drew Zulfiqar, the sword from Heaven gifted to him by the hand of the Prophet from the Angel Gabriel. Ali and his men marched on to the Baqee' Cemetery where the people had gathered.

The people of Medina watched as the Lion of God and his pride moved closer to them. Ali did not speak. His eyes spoke a thousand words. His sword glistened in the sun and told a tale of vengeance for God and His Prophet, and of a promise to his Lady of Light. His armor reminded them of what he defended and who he answered to.

"This is Ali ibn Abi Talib who has come in such a state… that if even one stone is turned from upon these graves, he will kill all of you!" one of the townspeople shouted out as Ali stood before them.

In those moments, Umar stepped forward with a band of his own men. He looked around at the graves in an irritable disapproval.

"O Ali! What is this that you have done?! We will indeed unearth the grave of Fatima and pray upon her!"

The Commander of the Faithful did not hesitate to reply. He grabbed Umar by the neck and slammed him to the ground. He hovered above him like a lion upon its prey and made it clear.

"O son of Sahhak! I sacrificed my rights out of fear that people would leave the faith. But as for desecrating the grave of Fatima, I swear by Allah in whose hands lies my life," Ali tightened his grip around Umar's neck while drawing his legendary sword.

"If you dare, I will quench the thirst of the earth with your blood! Do not do it and save yourself!"

Everyone stood still, not daring to move. Abu Bakr came forward barely touching the shoulder of Ali. He spoke softly,

"Please Ali, I beg of you, by the right of the Prophet and the One who is upon the High Heavens, leave Umar. We will not do that which displeases you."

Ali released his grip and let Umar go. He stood to his feet and peered upon the people. The message was clear. Ali endured all that he had, but this line was not to be crossed. Fatima's grave was to remain unknown, as she wished. They took her rights and desecrated her sanctity while she was alive. They would not be able to do so after her death.

CHAPTER 14

EPILOGUE

Firewood was brought to our house with the intention of burning it down along with its occupants.

– Lady Fatima

Many years after the tragedy of Lady Fatima, a poet would lament her sorrow with a few verses of poetry.

To what conditions should be buried in secret, the piece of al-Mustafa and her grave flattened...

Her sorrow was greater than any sorrow of man, and in the age her grave be in concealment...

So that people may not find track of it. Where is the sacred place that contains her grave?

The story of Fatima is surely not easy on the heart. It is a reality that could be difficult for some to reflect upon and contemplate. But it is a story weaved within the essence of the lovers and servants of Muhammad. Fatima lived a short, yet quintessential life, inspiring the hearts of men and women alike. It was through her that the legacy of Muhammad would continue and thrive. Through the sons of Fatima, his religion would live on to illuminate the darkness for humankind. Fatima's life and legacy, her death and tragedy, must be remembered. They ought to be honored, to keep aflame the lantern of salvation. And although her story is short, her memory is bold. Even if it is just for the few in your midst, let her story be told.

***

Perhaps, the walls of the house of Fatima cradled the family of Fatima a little closer after she departed. Perhaps, if the walls could speak, they would tell us of how a heartbroken Ali would whisper after Fatima, "The loss of a beloved is exile."

They may tell us of the time Ali summoned his dear brother Aqil, requesting his assistance as he searched for a noble lady, a descendant of heroes, to journey alongside him as a wife and partner, supporting Ali and protecting his children. The walls would tell us that she was the daughter of Hazim, that her name was also Fatima. Or it was, until Ali called out to her 'Oh Fatima', and her heart broke with grief as she witnessed the pain on the tender faces of the children as they remembered their beloved mother.

"Oh Ali, call me *Um Al-Baneen*," she would plead.

And a 'Mother of Sons' she certainly was, bearing four valiant sons to protect the children of the Lady of Light. Her immense love and devotion for Hasan and Husayn would stand the test of time, across the deserts of Arabia, where the flames that burned the door of Lady Fatima would one day rekindle themselves in the tent of her daughter, Lady Zaynab.

Until time unraveled those moments, forever inscribing them into pages and hearts, Ali lived his days serving, protecting, and patiently enduring until patience tired of his patience, and alive within him the words of his beloved Fatima.

"Let my death not dishearten you, you have to serve Islam and humanity for a long time to come, and let not my sufferings embitter your life, please promise me Ali."

Ali promised. For Fatima… the Flower of Life.

SELECT BIBLIOGRAPHY

Al-Ameen, Sayyid Muhsin. *Ayan al-Shia* (Beirut: Dar al-Ta'aruf lil-Matboo'at, 1983).

Abd Rabbih, Ahmad ibn Muhammad ibn. *al-ʿIqd al-Farīd*. (Beirut: Dār al-Kitāb al-ʿArabī, 1993).

Al-Akkad, Abbas Mahmoud. *'Abqariyet al-Imam* (Cairo: Nahdet Masr, 2003).

Al-Asfahani, Abu Na'eem. *Hiliyat al-Awliya'* (Cairo: 1932).

Al-'Askari, Sayyid Murtadha. *Ahadeeth Umm al-Mu'mineen Aisha* (Beirut: Al-Ghadeer, 1997).

Al-Atheer, Ali Ibn. *Usd al-Ghabah fi Marifat al-Sahabah* (Beirut: Dar Ibn Hazm, 2012).

Al-Atheer, Ali Ibn. *Al-Kamil fi al-Tareekh* (Beirut: Dar al-Kutub al-'Ilmiya, 1987).

Al-Balādhurī, ʾAḥmad ibn Yaḥyā. *Ansab al-Ashraf* (Beirut: Yutlabu Min F. Shataynir, 1978).

Chamseddine, Muhammad Mehdi. *The Course of History: A Study in the Peak of Eloquence* (USA: The Mainstay Foundation, 2016).

Al-Hadid, Izz al-Din ibn Abi. *Sharh Nahj al-Balagha*, ed. Muhammad Abu al-Fadl Ibrahim (Cairo: Isa al-Babi al-Halabi, 1959).

Al-Hindi, al-Muttaqi. *Kanz al-Ummal Fee Sunan al-Aqwal wa al-Af'al*, ed. Mahmud Umar al-Dumyati (Beirut: Dār al-Kutub al- 'Ilmīyah, 1998).

Hisham, Abu Muhammad Abdul Malik ibn. *Al-Seerah al-Nabawiyya* (Beirut: Dar al-Ma'rifa, 1982).

Hussein, Taha. *Al-Ftina al-Kubra* (Beirut: Dar al-Ma'aref, 2007).

Ibn Kathir. *Al-Sira Al-Nabawiyyah: The Life of the Prophet Muhammad*, Vol. 1, trans. by Professor Trevor Le Gassick (London: Garnet Publishers, 1998).

Al-Irbilī, 'Alī ibn 'Isā. *Kashf al-Ghumma fī Ma'rifat al-A'imma* (Beirut: Dār al-Adwā', 1985).

Lalljee, Yusuf. *Ali the Magnificent.* (Qom: Ansariyan Publications, 2004).

Al-Mufid, Shaykh. *Kitab Al-Irshad* (Beirut: Dar al-Mufid, 1993).

Al-Mufid, Shaykh. *Kitab Al-Irshad*, trans. I.K.A. Howard as *The Book of Guidance* (London: The Muhammadi Trust, 1981).

Al-Nesapuri, Al-Hakim. *Al-Mustadrak ala as-Saheehayn* (Beirut: Dar al-Ma'rifa, 1970).

Nicholson, Reynold Alleyne. A Literary History of the Arabs (Cambridge: Cambridge University Press 1930).

Al-Qarashi, Baqir Sharif. *The Life of Fatima Az-Zahra': The Principal of All Women, Study and Analysis*, trans. Sayyid Athar Husayn S.H. Rizvi (Qom: Ansariyan Publications, 2010).

Al-Qazwini, Sayyid Kadhim. *Fatimah al-Zahra: from the Cradle to the Grave*, trans. Tahir Ridha Jaffer (Tehran: World Organization for Islamic Services, 2015).

Al-Qummi, Shaykh Abbas. *House of Sorrows, the Life of Sayyidah Fatima al-Zahra and Her Grief*, trans. Aejaz Ali T. Bhujwala (Canada: Islamic Publishing House, 2010).

Al-Shiblanji, Mu'min ibn Hasan. *Nour al-Absar* (Qom: Radi Publishing, 1982).

Al-Tabari, Abu Jafar Muhammad ibn Jarir. *Tareekh al-Rusul wa al-Mulook*, translated as *The History of al-Tabari*, Vol. 9. "The Last Years of the Prophet: The Formation of the State A.D. 630-632/ A.H 8-11", trans. Ismail K. Poonawala (Albany: State University of New York Press, 1990).

Al-Tabari, Abu Jafar Muhammad ibn Jarir. *Tareekh al-Rusul wa al-Mulook*, translated as *The History of al-Tabari*, Vol. 10, "The Conquest of Arabia: The Riddah Wars A.D. 632-633/A.H. 11", trans. Fred Donner (Albany: State University of New York Press, 1993).

Al-Ṭūsī, Shaykh Abi Ja'far. Miṣbāḥ al-*Mutahajjid* (Beirut: Mu'assasat Fiqh al-Shi'a, 1991).

Wellhausen, Julius. *The Arab Kingdom and its Fall*, trans. by Margaret Graham Weir (Calcutta: University of Calcutta, 1927).

Printed in Great Britain
by Amazon